How To Enjoy Your Life And Your Job

Dale Carnegie

ISBN: 978-93-58049-81-7
eISBN: 978-93-58049-08-4

Publisher: Pharos Books (P) Ltd.
Plot No.-55, Main Mother Dairy Road
Pandav Nagar, East Delhi-110092
Phone: 011-40395855, +14049995474
WhatsApp: +91 8368220032
E-mail: sales@pharosbooks.in
Website: www.pharosbooks.in
First Edition: 2024

Printed By: Sushma Book Binding House, Okhla Industrial Area, Phase I, New Delhi-110020

How to Enjoy Your Life and Your Job
Dale Carnegie

Contents

How To Enjoy Your Life And Your Job

This book was authored by Dale Carnegi, who was also the author of the best selling "How to win friends and influence people", "How to stop worrying and start living" and many more self-help books.

The book narrates if one wishes to enjoy one's job, then one has to be co-operative to one's colleagues. And if we are not happy in our job, then we are only responsible for this. Therefore, we have to change our attitude.

One should love one's job whole-heartedly.

A quote says- "Choose such a job where you don't have to work for a single day."

The book provides many such techniques which will be helpful to you, so that you can enjoy your life too. You should be enthusiastic, maintain your originality and have patience in your job.

The book is self-development book, lays emphasis on our job.

Readers will surely start enjoying their jobs and thus life too. A must read book for all those interested in making life enjoyable and for self-development.

PART I

WIN FRIENDS AND INFLUENCE PEOPLE

1

HOW TO MAKE PEOPLE LIKE YOU INSTANTLY

I was waiting in line to register a letter in the post office at Thirty-third Street and Eighth Avenue in New York. I noticed that the clerk appeared to be bored with the job—weighing envelopes, handing out stamps, making change, issuing receipts—the same monotonous grind year after year. So I said to myself: "I am going to try to make that clerk like me. Obviously, to make him like me, I must say something nice, not about myself, but about him." So I asked myself, "What is there about him that I can honestly admire?" That is sometimes a hard question to answer, especially with strangers; but, in this case, it happened to be easy. I instantly saw something I admired no end.

So while he was weighing my envelope, I remarked with enthusiasm: "I certainly wish I had your head of hair."

He looked up, half-startled, his face beaming with smiles. "Well, it isn't as good as it used to be," he said modestly. I assured him that although it might have lost some of its pristine glory, nevertheless it was still magnificent. He was immensely pleased. We carried on a pleasant little conversation and the last thing he said to me was: "Many people have admired my hair."

I'll bet that person went out to lunch that day walking on air. I'll bet he went home that night and told his wife about it. I'll bet he looked in the mirror and said: "It is a beautiful head of hair."

I told this story once in public and a man asked me afterward: "What did you want to get out of him?"

What did I want to get out of him!!! What did I want to get out of him!!!

If we are so contemptibly selfish that we can't radiate a little happiness and pass on a bit of honest appreciation without trying to get something out of the other person in return—if our souls are no bigger than sour crab apples, we shall meet with the failure we so richly deserve.

Oh yes, I did want something out of that chap. I wanted something priceless. And I got it. I got the feeling that I had done something for him without his being able to do anything whatever in return for me. That is a feeling that flows and sings in your memory long after the incident is past.

There is one all-important law of human conduct. If we obey that law, we shall almost never get into trouble. In fact, that law, if obeyed, will bring us countless friends and constant happiness. But the very instant we break the law, we shall get into endless trouble. The law is this: *Always make the other person feel important.* John Dewey said that the desire to be important is the deepest urge in human nature; and William James said: "The deepest principle in human nature is the craving to be appreciated." As I have already pointed out, it is this urge that differentiates us from the animals. It is this urge that has been responsible for civilization itself.

Philosophers have been speculating on the rules of human relationships for thousands of years, and out of all that speculation, there has evolved only one important precept. It is not new. It is as old as history. Zoroaster taught it to his followers in Persia twenty-five hundred years ago. Confucius preached it in China twenty-four centuries ago. Lao-tse, the founder of Taoism, taught it to his disciples in the Valley of the Han twenty-five centuries ago. Buddha preached it on the bank of the Holy Ganges five hundred years before Christ. The sacred books of Hinduism taught it a thousand years before that.

Jesus taught it among the stony hills of Judea nineteen centuries ago. Jesus summed it up in one thought—probably the most important rule in the world: "Do unto others as you would have others do unto you."

You want the approval of those with whom you come in contact. You want recognition of your true worth. You want a feeling that you are important in your little world. You don't want to listen to cheap, insincere flattery, but you do crave sincere appreciation. You want your friends and associates to be, as Charles Schwab put it, "hearty in their approbation and lavish in their praise." All of us want that.

So let's obey the Golden Rule, and give unto others what we would have others give unto us.

How? When? Where? The answer is: All the time, everywhere.

David G. Smith of Eau Claire, Wisconsin, told one of our classes how he handled a delicate situation when he was asked to take charge of the refreshment booth at a charity concert.

"The night of the concert I arrived at the park and found two elderly ladies in a very bad humor standing next to the refreshment stand. Apparently each thought that she was in charge of this project. As I stood there pondering what to do, one of the members of the sponsoring committee appeared and handed me a cash box and thanked me for taking over the project. She introduced Rose and Jane as my helpers and then ran off.

"A great silence ensued. Realizing that the cash box was a symbol of authority (of sorts), I gave the box to Rose and explained that I might not be able to keep the money straight and that if she took care of it I would feel better. I then suggested to Jane that she show two teenagers who had been assigned to refreshments how to operate the soda machine, and I asked her to be responsible for that part of the project.

"The evening was very enjoyable, with Rose happily counting the money, Jane supervising the teenagers, and me enjoying the concert."

You don't have to wait until you are ambassador to France or chairman of the Clambake Committee of your lodge before you use this philosophy of appreciation. You can work magic with it almost every day.

If, for example, the waitress brings us mashed potatoes when we have ordered French fries, let's say: "I'm sorry to trouble you, but I prefer French fries." She'll probably reply, "No trouble at all" and will be glad to change the potatoes, because we have shown respect for her.

Little phrases such as "I'm sorry to trouble you," "Would you be so kind as to?" "Won't you please?" "Would you mind?" "Thank you"— little courtesies like these relieve the monotonous grind of everyday life— and, incidentally, they are the hallmark of good breeding.

The unvarnished truth is that almost all the people you meet feel themselves superior to you in some way, and a sure way to their hearts is to let them realize in some subtle way that you recognize their importance, and recognize it sincerely.

Remember what Emerson said: "Every man I meet is my superior in some way. In that, I learn of him."

And the pathetic part of it is that frequently those who have the least justification for a feeling of achievement bolster their egos by a show of tumult and conceit that is truly nauseating. As Shakespeare put it: "...man, proud man / Drest in a little brief authority / ...Plays such fantastic tricks before high heaven / As make the angels weep."

I am going to tell you how business people in my own courses have applied these principles with remarkable results. Let's take the case of a Connecticut attorney (because of his relatives he prefers not to have his name mentioned).

Shortly after joining the course, Mr. R—drove to Long Island with his wife to visit some of her relatives. She left him to chat with an old aunt of hers and then rushed off by herself to visit some of the younger relatives. Since he soon had to give a speech professionally on how he applied the principles of appreciation, he thought he would gain some worthwhile experience talking with the elderly lady. So he looked around the house to see what he could honestly admire.

"This house was built about 1890, wasn't it?" he inquired.

"Yes," she replied, "that is precisely the year it was built."

"It reminds me of the house I was born in," he said. "It's beautiful. Well built. Roomy. You know, they don't build houses like this anymore."

"You're right," the old lady agreed. "The young folks nowadays don't care for beautiful homes. All they want is a small apartment, and then they go off gadding about in their automobiles.

"This is a dream house," she said in a voice vibrating with tender memories. "This house was built with love. My husband and I dreamed about it for years before we built it. We didn't have an architect. We planned it all ourselves."

She showed Mr. R about the house, and he expressed his hearty admiration for the beautiful treasures she had picked up in her travels and cherished over a lifetime— paisley shawls, an old English tea set, Wedgwood china, French beds and chairs, Italian paintings, and silk draperies that had once hung in a French chateau.

After showing Mr. R—through the house, she took him out to the garage. There, jacked up on blocks, was a Packard car—in mint condition.

"My husband bought that car for me shortly before he passed on," she said softly. "I have never ridden in it since his death... You appreciate nice things, and I'm going to give this car to you."

"Why, Aunty," he said, "you overwhelm me. I appreciate your generosity, of course; but I couldn't possibly accept it. I'm not even a relative of yours. I have a new car, and you have many relatives who would like to have that Packard."

"Relatives!" she exclaimed. "Yes, I have relatives who are just waiting till I die so they can get that car. But they are not going to get it."

"If you don't want to give it to them, you can very easily sell it to a secondhand dealer," he told her.

"Sell it!" she cried. "Do you think I would sell this car? Do you think I could stand to see strangers riding up and down the street in that car—that car that my husband bought for me? I wouldn't dream of selling it. I'm going to give it to you. You appreciate beautiful things."

He tried to get out of accepting the car, but he couldn't without hurting her feelings.

This lady, left all alone in a big house with her paisley shawls, her French antiques, and her memories, was starving for a little recognition. She had once been young and beautiful and sought-after. She had once built a house warm with love and had collected things from all over Europe to make it beautiful. Now, in the isolated loneliness of old age, she craved a little human warmth, a little genuine appreciation—and no one gave it to her. And when she found it, like a spring in the desert, her gratitude couldn't adequately express itself with anything less than the gift of her cherished Packard.

Let's take another case: Donald M. McMahon, who was superintendent of Lewis and Valentine, nurserymen and landscape architects in Rye, New York, related this incident:

"Shortly after I attended the talk on 'How to Win Friends and Influence People,' I was landscaping the estate of a famous judge. The owner came out to give me a few instructions about where he wished to plant a mass of rhododendrons and azaleas.

"I said, 'Judge, you have a lovely hobby. I've been admiring your beautiful dogs. I understand you win a lot of blue ribbons every year at the show in Madison Square Garden.'

"The effect of this little expression of appreciation was striking.

"'Yes,' the judge replied, 'I do have a lot of fun with my dogs. Would you like to see my kennel?'

"He spent almost an hour showing me his dogs and the prizes they had won. He even brought out their pedigrees and explained about the bloodlines responsible for such beauty and intelligence.

"Finally, turning to me, he asked: 'Do you have any small children?'

"'Yes, I do,' I replied. 'I have a son.'

"'Well, wouldn't he like a puppy?' the judge inquired.

"'Oh, yes, he'd be tickled pink.'

"'All right, I'm going to give him one,' the judge announced.

"He started to tell me how to feed the puppy. Then he paused. 'You'll forget it if I tell you. I'll write it out.' So the judge went in the house, typed out the pedigree and feeding instructions, and gave me a puppy worth several hundred dollars and one hour and fifteen minutes of his valuable time largely because I had expressed my honest admiration for his hobby and achievements."

George Eastman, of Kodak fame, invented the transparent film that made motion pictures possible, amassed a fortune of a hundred million dollars, and made himself one of the most famous businessmen on earth. Yet in spite of all these tremendous accomplishments, he craved a little recognition even as you and I.

To illustrate: When Eastman was building the Eastman School of Music and also Kilbourn Hall in Rochester, James Adamson, then president of the Superior Seating Company of New York, wanted to get the order to supply the theater chairs for these buildings. Phoning the architect, Mr. Adamson made an appointment to see Mr. Eastman in Rochester.

When Adamson arrived, the architect said: "I know you want to get this order, but I can tell you right now that you won't stand a ghost of a show if you take more than five minutes of George Eastman's time. He is a strict disciplinarian. He is very busy. So tell your story quickly and get out."

Adamson was prepared to do just that.

When he was ushered into the room he saw Mr. Eastman bending over a pile of papers at his desk. Presently, Mr. Eastman looked up, removed his glasses, and walked toward the architect and Mr. Adamson, saying: "Good morning, gentlemen, what can I do for your?"

The architect introduced them, and then Mr. Adamson said: "While we've been waiting for you, Mr. Eastman, I've been admiring your office. I wouldn't mind working in a room like this myself. I'm in the interior-woodworking business, and I never saw a more beautiful office in all my life.

George Eastman replied: "You remind me of something I had almost forgotten. It is beautiful, isn't it? I enjoyed it a great deal when it was first built. But I come down here now with a lot of other things on my mind and sometimes don't even see the room for weeks at a time."

Adamson walked over and rubbed his hand across a panel. "This is English oak, isn't it? A little different in texture from Italian oak."

"Yes," Eastman replied. "Imported English oak. It was selected for me by a friend who specializes in fine woods."

Then Eastman showed him about the room, commenting on the proportions, the coloring, the hand carving, and other efforts he had helped to plan and execute.

While drifting about the room, admiring the woodwork, they paused before a window, and George Eastman, in his modest, soft-spoken way, pointed out some of the institutions through which he was trying to help humanity: the University of Rochester, the General Hospital, the Homeopathic Hospital, the Friendly Home, the Children's Hospital. Mr. Adamson congratulated him warmly on the idealistic way he was using his wealth to alleviate the sufferings of humanity. Presently, George Eastman unlocked a glass case and pulled out the first camera he had ever owned—an invention he had bought from an Englishman.

Adamson questioned him at length about his early struggles to get started in business, and Mr. Eastman spoke with real feeling about the poverty of his childhood, telling how his widowed mother had kept a boarding house while he clerked in an insurance office. The terror of poverty haunted him day and night, and he resolved to make enough money so that his mother wouldn't have to work. Mr. Adamson drew him out with further questions and listened, absorbed, while he related the story of his experiments with dry photographic plates. He told how he had worked in an office all day, and sometimes experimented all night, taking only brief naps while the chemicals were working and sleeping in his clothes for seventy-two hours at a stretch.

James Adamson had been ushered into Eastman's office at ten-fifteen and had been warned that he must not take more than five minutes; but an hour passed, then two hours passed. And they were still talking.

Finally, George Eastman turned to Adamson and said, "The last time I was in Japan I bought some chairs, brought them home, and put them in my sun porch. But the sun peeled the paint, so I went downtown the other day and bought some paint and painted the chairs myself. Would you like to see what sort of a job I can do painting chairs?

All right. Come up to my home and have lunch with me and I'll show you."

After lunch, Mr. Eastman showed Adamson the chairs he had brought from Japan. They weren't worth more than a few dollars, but George Eastman, now a multimillionaire, was proud of them because he himself had painted them.

The order for the seats amounted to ninety thousand dollars. Who do you suppose got the order—James Adamson or one of his competitors? From the time of this story until Mr. Eastman's death, he and James Adamson were close friends.

Claude Marais, a restaurant owner in Rouen, France, used this principle and saved his restaurant the loss of a key employee. This woman had been in his employ for five years and was a vital link between M. Marais and his staff of twenty-one people. He was shocked to receive a registered letter from her advising him of her resignation.

M. Marais reported: "I was very surprised and, even more, disappointed, because I was under the impression that I had been fair to her and receptive to her needs. Inasmuch as she was a friend as well as an employee, I probably had taken her too much for granted and maybe was even more demanding of her than of other employees.

"I could not, of course, accept this resignation without some explanation. I took her aside and said, 'Paulette, you must understand that I cannot accept your resignation. You mean a great deal to me and to this company, and you are as important to the success of this restaurant as I am.' I repeated this in front of the entire staff, and I invited her to my home and reiterated my confidence in her with my family present.

"Paulette withdrew her resignation, and today I can rely on her as never before. I frequently reinforce this by expressing my appreciation for what she does and showing her how important she is to me and to the restaurant."

"Talk to people about themselves," said Disraeli, one of the shrewdest men who ever ruled the British Empire. "Talk to people about themselves and they will listen for hours."

Always Make the Other Person Feel Important

* * *

Inaction breeds doubt and fear. Action breeds confidence and courage. If you want to conquer fear, do not sit home and think about it. Go out and get busy.

– Dale Carnegie

2

DO THIS AND YOU'LL BE WELCOME ANYWHERE

Why read this book to find out how to win friends? Why not study the technique of the greatest winner of friends the world has ever known? Who is he? You may meet him tomorrow coming down the street. When you get within ten feet of him, he will begin to wag his tail. If you stop and pat him, he will almost jump out of his skin to show you how much he likes you. And you know that behind this show of affection on his part, there are no ulterior motives: he doesn't want to sell you any real estate, and he doesn't want to marry you.

Did you ever stop to think that a dog is the only animal that doesn't have to work for a living? A hen has to lay eggs, a cow has to give milk, and a canary has to sing. But a dog makes his living by giving you nothing but love.

When I was five years old, my father bought a little yellow-haired pup for fifty cents. He was the light and joy of my childhood. Every afternoon about four-thirty, he would sit in the front yard with his beautiful eyes staring steadfastly at the path, and as soon as he heard my voice or saw me swinging my dinner pail through the buck brush, he was off like a shot, racing breathlessly up the hill to greet me with leaps of joy and barks of sheer ecstasy.

Tippy was my constant companion for five years. Then one tragic night—I shall never forget it—he was killed within ten feet of me, killed by lightning. Tippy's death was the tragedy of my boyhood.

You never read a book on psychology, Tippy. You didn't need to. You knew by some divine instinct that you can make more friends in two months by becoming genuinely interested in other people than you can in two years by trying to get other people interested in you. Let me repeat that. You can make more friends in two months by becoming interested in other people than you can in two years by trying to get other people interested in you.

Yet I know and you know people who blunder through life trying to wigwag other people into becoming interested in them.

Of course, it doesn't work. People are not interested in you. They are not interested in me. They are interested in themselves—morning, noon, and after dinner.

The New York Telephone Company made a detailed study of telephone conversations to find out which word is the most frequently used. You have guessed it: it is the personal pronoun "I." "I." "I." It was used 3,900 times in 500 telephone conversations. "I." "I." "I." "I."

When you see a group photograph that you are in, whose picture do you look for first?

If we merely try to impress people and get people interested in us, we will never have many true, sincere friends. Friends, real friends, are not made that way.

Napoleon tried it, and in his last meeting with Josephine he said: "Josephine, I have been as fortunate as any man ever was on this earth; and yet, at this hour, you are the only person in the world on whom I can rely." And historians doubt that he could rely even on her.

I once took a course in short-story writing at New York University, and during that course the editor of a leading magazine talked to our class. He said he could pick up any one of the dozens of stories that drifted across his desk every day and after reading a few paragraphs he could feel whether or not the author liked people. "If the author doesn't like people," he said, "people won't like his or her stories."

This hard-boiled editor stopped twice in the course of his talk on fiction writing and apologized for preaching a sermon. "I am telling you," he said, "the same things your preacher would tell you, but remember, you have to be interested in people if you want to be a successful writer of stories."

If that is true of writing fiction, you can be sure it is true of dealing with people face-to-face.

I spent an evening in the dressing room of Howard Thurston the last time he appeared on Broadway— Thurston was the acknowledged dean of magicians. For forty years he had traveled all over the world, time and again, creating illusions, mystifying audiences, and making people gasp with astonishment. More than 60 million people had paid admission to his show, and he had made almost $2 million in profit.

I asked Mr. Thurston to tell me the secret of his success. His schooling certainly had nothing to do with it, for he ran away from home as a small boy, became a hobo, rode in boxcars, slept in haystacks, begged his food from door to door, and learned to read by looking out of boxcars at signs along the railway.

Did he have a superior knowledge of magic? No, he told me hundreds of books had been written about legerdemain and scores of people knew as much about it as he did. But he had two things that the others didn't have. First, he had the ability to put his personality across the footlights. He was a master showman. He knew human nature. Everything he did, every gesture, every intonation of his voice, every lifting of an eyebrow had been carefully rehearsed, and his actions were timed to split seconds. But, in addition to that, Thurston had a genuine interest in people. He told me that many magicians would look at the audience and say to themselves, "Well, there is a bunch of suckers out there, a bunch of hicks; I'll fool them all right." But Thurston's method was totally different. He told me that every time he went on stage he said to himself: "I am grateful because these people came to see me. They make it possible for me to make my living in a very agreeable way. I'm going to give them the very best I possibly can."

He declared he never stepped in front of the footlights without first saying to himself over and over: "I love my audience. I love my audience." Ridiculous? Absurd? You are privileged to think anything you like. I am merely passing it on to you without comment as a recipe used by one of the most famous magicians of all time.

George Dyke of North Warren, Pennsylvania, was forced to retire from his service station business after thirty years when a new highway was constructed over the site of his station. It wasn't long before the idle days of retirement began to bore him, so he started filling in his time trying to play music on his old fiddle. Soon he was traveling the area to listen to music and talk with many of the accomplished fiddlers. In his humble and friendly way he became generally interested in learning the background and interests of every musician he met. Although he was not a great fiddler himself, he made many friends in this pursuit. He attended competitions and soon became known to the country music fans in the eastern part of the United States as "Uncle George, the Fiddle Scraper from Kinzua County." When we heard Uncle George, he was seventy-two and enjoying every minute of his life. By having a sustained interest in other people, he created a new life for himself at a time when most people consider their productive years over.

That, too, was one of the secrets of Theodore Roosevelt's astonishing popularity. Even his servants loved him. His valet, James E. Amos, wrote a book about him entitled *Theodore Roosevelt, Hero to His Valet.* In that book Amos relates this illuminating incident:

> My wife one time asked the President about a bobwhite. She had never seen one and he described it to her fully. Sometime later, the telephone at our cottage rang. [Amos and his wife lived in a little cottage on the Roosevelt estate at Oyster Bay.] My wife answered it and it was Mr. Roosevelt himself. He had called her, he said, to tell her that there was a bobwhite outside her window and that if she would look out she might see it. Little things like that were so characteristic of him. Whenever he went by our cottage, even though we were out of sight, we would hear him call out: "Oo-oo-oo, Annie?" or "Oo-oo-oo, James!" It was just a friendly greeting as he went by.

How could employees keep from liking a man like that? How could anyone keep from liking him?

Roosevelt called at the White House one day when the President and Mrs. Taft were away. His honest liking for humble people was shown by the fact that he greeted all the old White House servants by name, even the scullery maids.

"When he saw Alice, the kitchen maid," writes Archie Butt, "he asked her if she still made corn bread. Alice told him that she sometimes made it for the servants, but no one ate it upstairs.

"'They show bad taste,' Roosevelt boomed, 'and I'll tell the President so when I see him.'

"Alice brought a piece to him on a plate, and he went over to the office eating it as he went and greeting gardeners and laborers as he passed...

"He addressed each person just as he had addressed them in the past. Ike Hoover, who had been head usher at the White House for forty years, said with tears in his eyes, 'It is the only happy day we had in nearly two years, and not one of us would exchange it for a hundred- dollar bill.'"

The same concern for the seemingly unimportant people helped sales representative Edward M. Sykes, Jr., of Chatham, New Jersey, retain an account. "Many years ago," he reported, "I called on customers for Johnson and Johnson in the Massachusetts area. One account was a drug store in Hingham. Whenever I went into this store I would always talk to the soda clerk and sales clerk for a few minutes before talking to the owner to obtain his order. One day I went up to the owner of the store, and he told me to leave as he was not interested in buying J&J products anymore because he felt they were concentrating their activities on food and discount stores to the detriment of the small drugstore. I left with my tail between my legs and drove around the town for several hours. Finally, I decided to go back and try at least to explain our position to the owner of the store.

"When I returned I walked in and as usual said hello to the soda clerk and sales clerk. When I walked up to the owner, he smiled at me and welcomed me back. He then gave me double the usual order. I looked at him with surprise and asked him what had happened since my visit only a few hours earlier. He pointed to the young man at the soda fountain and said that after I had left, the boy had come over and said that I was one of the few salespeople who called on the store who even bothered to say hello to him and to the others in the store. He told the owner that if any salesperson deserved his business, it was I. The owner agreed and remained a loyal customer. I never forgot that to be genuinely interested in other people is a most important quality for a salesperson to possess—for any person, for that matter."

I have discovered from personal experience that one can win the attention and time and cooperation of even the most sought-after people by becoming genuinely interested in them. Let me illustrate.

Years ago I conducted a course in fiction writing at the Brooklyn Institute of Arts and Sciences, and we wanted such distinguished and busy authors as Kathleen Norris, Fannie Hurst, Ida Tarbell, Albert Payson Terhune, and Rupert Hughes to come to Brooklyn and give us the benefit of their experience. So we wrote them, saying we admired their work and were deeply interested in getting their advice and learning the secrets of their success.

Each of these letters was signed by about 150 students. We said we realized that these authors were busy—too busy to prepare a lecture. So we enclosed a list of questions for them to answer about themselves and their methods of work. They liked that. Who wouldn't like it? So they left their homes and traveled to Brooklyn to give us a helping hand.

By using the same method, I persuaded Leslie M. Shaw, secretary of the treasury in Theodore Roosevelt's cabinet; George W. Wickersham, attorney general in Taft's cabinet; William Jennings Bryan; Franklin D. Roosevelt; and many other prominent men to come to talk to the students of my courses in public speaking.

All of us, be we workers in a factory, clerks in an office, or even a king upon his throne—all of us like people who admire us. Take the German kaiser, for example. At the close of World War I, he was probably the most savagely and universally despised man on this earth. Even his own nation turned against him when he fled over into Holland to save his neck. The hatred against him was so intense that millions of people would have loved to tear him limb from limb or burn him at the stake. In the midst of all this forest fire of fury, one little boy wrote the kaiser a simple, sincere letter glowing with kindliness and admiration. This little boy said that no matter what the others thought, he would always love Wilhelm as his emperor. The kaiser was deeply touched by his letter and invited the little boy to come see him. The boy came, so did his mother—and the kaiser married her. That little boy didn't need to read a book on how to win friends and influence people. He knew how instinctively.

If we want to make friends, let's put ourselves out to do things for other people—things that require time, energy, unselfishness, and thoughtfulness. When the Duke of Windsor was Prince of Wales, he was scheduled to tour South America, and before he started out on that tour he spent months studying Spanish so that he could make public talks in the language of the country; and the South Americans loved him for it.

For years I made it a point to find out the birthdays of my friends. How? Although I haven't the foggiest bit of faith in astrology, I began by asking the other party whether he believed the date of one's birth has anything to do with character and disposition. I then asked him or her to tell me the month and day of birth. If he or she said November 24, for example, I kept repeating to myself, "November 24, November 24." The minute my friend's back was turned, I wrote down the name and birthday and later would transfer it to a birthday book. At the beginning of each year, I had these birthday dates scheduled in my calendar pad so that they came to my attention automatically. When the natal day arrived, there was my letter or telegram. What a hit it made! I was frequently the only person on earth who remembered.

If we want to make friends, let's greet people with animation and enthusiasm. When somebody calls you on the telephone use the same psychology. Say "Hello" in tones that bespeak how pleased you are to have the person call. Many companies train their telephone operators to greet all callers in a tone that radiates interest and enthusiasm. The callers feel the company is concerned about them. Let's remember that when we answer the telephone tomorrow.

Showing a genuine interest in others not only wins friends for you, but may develop in its customers a loyalty to your company. In an issue of the publication of the National Bank of North America of New York, the following letter from Madeline Rosedale, a depositor, was published:

"I would like you to know how much I appreciate your staff. Everyone is so courteous, polite, and helpful. What a pleasure it is, after waiting in a long line, to have the teller greet you pleasantly.

"Last year my mother was hospitalized for five months. Frequently I went to Marie Petrucello, a teller. She was concerned about my mother and inquired about her progress."

Is there any doubt that Mrs. Rosedale will continue to use this bank?

Charles R. Walters, of one of the large banks in New York City, was assigned to prepare a confidential report on a certain corporation. He knew of only one person who possessed the facts he needed so urgently. As Mr. Walters was ushered into the president's office, a young woman stuck her head through a door and told the president that she didn't have any stamps for him that day.

"I am collecting stamps for my twelve-year-old son," the president explained to Mr. Walters.

Mr. Walters stated his mission and began asking questions. The president was vague, general, nebulous. He didn't want to talk, and apparently nothing could persuade him to talk. The interview was brief and barren.

"Frankly, I didn't know what to do," Mr. Walters said as he related the story to the class. "Then I remembered what his secretary had said to him—stamps, twelve-year- old son... And I also recalled that the foreign department of our bank collected stamps—stamps taken from letters pouring in from every continent washed by the seven seas.

"The next afternoon I called on this man and sent in word that I had some stamps for his boy. Was I ushered in with enthusiasm? Yes sir. He couldn't have shaken my hand with more enthusiasm if he had been running for Congress. He radiated smiles and good will. 'My George will love this one,' he kept saying as he fondled the stamps. 'And look at this! This is a treasure.'

"We spent half an hour talking stamps and looking at a picture of his boy, and he then devoted more than an hour of his time to giving me every bit of information I wanted—without my even suggesting that he do it. He told me all he knew, and then called in his subordinates and questioned them. He telephoned some of his associates. He loaded me down with facts, figures, reports, and correspondence. In the parlance of newspaper reporters, I had a scoop."

Here is another illustration:

C. M. Knaphle, Jr., of Philadelphia, had tried for years to sell fuel to a large chain-store organization. But the chain-store company continued to purchase its fuel from an out-of-town dealer and haul it right past the door of Knaphle's office. Mr. Knaphle made a speech one night before one of my classes, pouring out his hot wrath upon chain stores, branding them as a curse on the nation.

And still he wondered why he couldn't sell them.

I suggested that he try different tactics. To put it briefly, this is what happened. We staged a debate between members of the course on whether the spread of the chain Store is doing the country more harm than good.

Knaphle, at my suggestion, took the negative side; he agreed to defend the chain stores, and then went straight to an executive of the chain-store organization that he despised and said: "I am not here to try to sell fuel. I have come to ask you to do me a favor." He then told about his debate and said, "I have come to you for help because I can't think of anyone else who would be more capable of giving me the facts I want. I'm anxious to win this debate, and I'll deeply appreciate whatever help you can give me."

Here is the rest of the story in Mr. Knaphle's own words:

> "I had asked this man for precisely one minute of his time. It was with this understanding that he consented to see me. After I had stated my case, he motioned me to a chair and talked to me for exactly one hour and forty-seven minutes. He called in another executive who had written a book about chain stores. He wrote to the National Chain Store Association and secured for me a copy of a debate on the subject. He feels that the chain store is rendering a real service to humanity. He is proud of what he is doing for hundreds of communities. His eyes fairly glowed as he talked, and I must confess that he opened my eyes to things I had never dreamed of. He changed my whole mental attitude.
>
> "As I was leaving, he walked with me to the door, put his arm around my shoulder, wished me well in my debate, and asked me to stop in and see him again and let him know how I made out. The last words he said to me were: 'Please see me again later in the spring. I should like to place an order with you for fuel.'
>
> "To me that was almost a miracle. Here he was offering to buy fuel without my even suggesting it. I had made more headway in two hours by becoming genuinely interested in him and his problems than I could have made in ten years trying to get him interested in me and my product."

You didn't discover a new truth, Mr. Knaphle, for a long time ago, a hundred years before Christ was born, a Roman poet, Publilius Syrus, remarked: "We are interested in others when they are interested in us."

A show of interest, as with every other principle of human relations, must be sincere. It must pay off not only for the person showing the interest, but for the person receiving the attention. It is a two-way street— both parties benefit.

Martin Ginsberg, who took our course in Long Island, New York, reported how the special interest a nurse took in him profoundly affected his life:

"It was Thanksgiving Day and I was ten years old. I was in a welfare ward of a city hospital and was scheduled to undergo major orthopedic surgery the next day. I knew that I could only look forward to months of confinement, convalescence, and pain. My father was dead; my mother and I lived alone in a small apartment and we were on welfare. My mother was unable to visit me that day.

"As the day went on, I became overwhelmed with the feeling of loneliness, despair, and fear. I knew my mother was home alone worrying about me, not having anyone to be with, not having anyone to eat with, and not even having enough money to afford a Thanksgiving Day dinner.

"The tears welled up in my eyes, and I stuck my head under the pillow and pulled the covers over it. I cried silently, but oh so bitterly, so much that my body racked with pain.

"A young student nurse heard my sobbing and came over to me. She took the covers off my face and started wiping my tears. She told me how lonely she was, having to work that day and not being able to be with her family. She asked me whether I would have dinner with her. She brought two trays of food: sliced turkey, mashed potatoes, cranberry sauce, and ice cream for dessert. She talked to me and tried to calm my fears. Even though she was scheduled to go off duty at 4:00 p.m., she stayed on her own time until almost 11:00 p.m. She played games with me, talked to me, and stayed with me until I finally fell asleep.

"Many Thanksgivings have come and gone since I was ten, but one never passes without my remembering that particular one and my feelings of frustration, fear, loneliness, and the warmth and tenderness of the stranger who somehow made it all bearable."

If you want others to like you, if you want to develop real friendships, if you want to help others at the same time as you help yourself, keep this principle in mind:

If We Want to Make Friends, Let's Greet People with Animation and Enthusiasm

* * *

Keep on raging - to stop the aging.

– Dale Carnegie

3

HOW TO DEAL WITH PEOPLE

There is only one way under high heaven to get anybody to do anything. Did you ever stop to think of that? Yes, just one way. And that is by making the other person want to do it.

Remember, there is no other way.

Of course, you can make someone want to give you his watch by sticking a revolver in his ribs. You can make your employees give you cooperation—until your back is turned—by threatening to fire them. You can make a child do what you want it to do by a whip or a threat. But these crude methods have sharply undesirable repercussions.

The only way I can get you to do anything is by giving you what you want.

What do you want?

Sigmund Freud said that everything you and I do springs from two motives: the sex urge and the desire to be great.

John Dewey, one of Americas most profound philosophers, phrased it a bit differently. Dr. Dewey said that the deepest urge in human nature is "the desire to be important." Remember that phrase: "the desire to be important." It is significant. You are going to hear a lot about it in this book.

What do you want? Not many things, but the few things that you do wish, you crave with an insistence that will not be denied. Some of the things most people want include:

1. Health and the preservation of life
2. Food
3. Sleep
4. Money and the things money will buy
5. Life in the hereafter
6. Sexual gratification
7. The well-being of our children
8. A feeling of importance

Almost all these wants are usually gratified—all except one. But there is one longing—almost as deep, almost as imperious, as the desire for food or sleep—that is seldom gratified. It is what Freud calls "the desire to be great." It is what Dewey calls "the desire to be important."

Lincoln once began a letter saying: "Everybody likes a compliment." William James said: "The deepest principle in human nature is the craving to be appreciated." He didn't speak, mind you, of the "wish" or the "desire" or the "longing" to be appreciated. He said the "craving" to be appreciated.

Here is a gnawing and unfaltering human hunger, and the rare individual who honestly satisfies this heart hunger will hold people in the palm of his or her hand and "even the undertaker will be sorry when he dies."

The desire for a feeling of importance is one of the chief distinguishing differences between mankind and the animals. To illustrate: When I was a farm boy out in Missouri, my father bred fine Duroc-Jersey hogs and pedigreed white-faced cattle. We used to exhibit our hogs and white-faced cattle at the country fairs and livestock shows throughout the Middle West. We won first prizes by the score. My father pinned his blue ribbons on a sheet of white muslin, and when friends or visitors came to the house, he would get out the long sheet of muslin. He would hold one end and I would hold the other while he exhibited the blue ribbons.

The hogs didn't care about the ribbons they had won. But Father did. These prizes gave him a feeling of importance.

If our ancestors hadn't had this flaming urge for a feeling of importance, civilization would have been impossible. Without it, we should have been just about like animals.

It was this desire for a feeling of importance that inspired Dickens to write his immortal novels. This desire inspired Sir Christopher Wren to design his symphonies in stone. This desire made Rockefeller amass millions that he never spent! And this same desire made the richest family in your town build a house far too large for its requirements.

This desire makes you want to wear the latest styles, drive the latest cars, and talk about your brilliant children.

It is this desire that lures many boys and girls into joining gangs and engaging in criminal activities. The average young criminal, according to E. P. Mulrooney, one-time police commissioner of New York, is filled with ego, and his first request after arrest is for those lurid newspapers that make him out a hero. The disagreeable prospect of serving time seems remote so long as he can gloat over his likeness sharing space with pictures of sports figures, movie and television stars, and politicians.

If you tell me how you get your feeling of importance, I'll tell you what you are. That determines your character. That is the most significant thing about you. For example, John D. Rockefeller got his feeling of importance by giving money to erect a modern hospital in Peking, China, to care for millions of poor people whom he had never seen and never would see. Dillinger, on the other hand, got his feeling of importance by being a bandit, a bank robber and killer. When the FBI agents were hunting him, he dashed into a farmhouse up in Minnesota and said, "I'm Dillinger!" He was proud of the fact that he was Public Enemy Number One. "I'm not going to hurt you, but I'm Dillinger!" he said.

Yes, the one significant difference between Dillinger and Rockefeller is how they got their feeling of importance.

History sparkles with amusing examples of famous people struggling for a feeling of importance. Even George Washington wanted to be called "His Mightiness, the President of the United States"; and Columbus pleaded for the title "Admiral of the Ocean and Viceroy of India." Catherine the Great refused to open letters that were not addressed to "Her Imperial Majesty"; and Mrs. Lincoln, in the White House, turned upon Mrs. Grant like a tigress and shouted, "How dare you be seated in my presence until I invite you!"

Our millionaires helped finance Admiral Byrd's expedition to the Antarctic in 1928 with the understanding that ranges of icy mountains would be named after them; and Victor Hugo aspired to have nothing less than the city of Paris renamed in his honor. Even Shakespeare, mightiest of the mighty, tried to add luster to his name by procuring a coat of arms for his family.

People sometimes become invalids in order to win sympathy and attention, and get a feeling of importance. For example, take Mrs. McKinley. She got a feeling of importance by forcing her husband, the President of the United States, to neglect important affairs of state while he reclined on the bed beside her for hours at a time, his arm about her, soothing her to sleep. She fed her gnawing desire for attention by insisting that he remain with her while she was having her teeth fixed, and once created a stormy scene when he had to leave her alone with the dentist while he kept an appointment with John Hay, his secretary of state.

The writer Mary Roberts Rinehart once told me of a bright, vigorous young woman who became, an invalid in order to get a feeling of importance. "One day," said Mrs. Rinehart, "this woman had been obliged to face something, her age perhaps. The lonely years were stretching ahead and there was little left for her to anticipate.

"She took to her bed; and for ten years her old mother traveled to the third floor and back, carrying trays, nursing her. Then one day the old mother, weary with service, lay down and died. For some weeks, the invalid languished; then she got up, put on her clothing, and resumed living again."

Some authorities declare that people may actually go insane in order to find, in the dreamland of insanity, the feeling of importance that has been denied them in the harsh world of reality. There are more patients suffering from mental diseases in the United States than from all other diseases combined.

What is the cause of insanity?

Nobody can answer such a sweeping question, but we know that certain diseases, such as syphilis, break down and destroy the brain cells and result in insanity. In fact, about one-half of all mental diseases can be attributed to such physical causes as brain lesions, alcohol, toxins, and injuries. But the other half—and this is the appalling part of the story—the other half of the people who go insane apparently have nothing organically wrong with their brain cells. In post-mortem examinations, when their brain tissues are studied under the highest-powered microscopes, these tissues are found to be apparently just as healthy as yours and mine.

Why do these people go insane?

I put that question to the head physician of one of our most important psychiatric hospitals. This doctor, who has received the highest honors and the most coveted awards for his knowledge of this subject, told me frankly that he didn't know why people went insane. Nobody knows for sure. But he did say that many people who go insane find in insanity a feeling of importance that they were unable to achieve in the world of reality. Then he told me this story:

"I have a patient right now whose marriage proved to be a tragedy. She wanted love, sexual gratification, children, and social prestige, but life blasted all her hopes. Her husband didn't love her. He refused even to eat with her and forced her to serve his meals in his room upstairs. She had no children, no social standing. She went insane; and, in her imagination, she divorced her husband and resumed her maiden name. She now believes she has married into English aristocracy, and she insists on being called Lady Smith.

"And as for children, she imagines now that she has had a new child every night. Each time I call on her she says: 'Doctor, I had a baby last night.'"

Life once wrecked all her dream ships on the sharp rocks of reality; but in the sunny, fantasy isles of insanity, all her barkentines race into port with canvas billowing and winds singing through the sails.

Tragic? Oh, I don't know. Her physician said to me: "If I could stretch out my hand and restore her sanity, I wouldn't do it. She's much happier as she is."

If some people are so hungry for a feeling of importance that they actually go insane to get it, imagine what miracle you and I can achieve by giving people honest appreciation this side of insanity.

One of the first people in American business to be paid a salary of over a million dollars a year (when there was no income tax and a person earning fifty dollars a week was considered well off) was Charles Schwab. He had been picked by Andrew Carnegie to become the first president of the newly formed United States Steel Company in 1921, when Schwab was only thirty-eight years old. (Schwab later left U.S. Steel to take over the then-troubled Bethlehem Steel Company, and he rebuilt it into one of the most profitable companies in America.)

Why did Andrew Carnegie pay a million dollars a year, or more than three thousand dollars a day, to Charles Schwab? Why? Because Schwab was a genius? No. Because he knew more about the manufacture of steel than other people? Nonsense. Charles Schwab told me himself that he had many men working for him who knew more about the manufacture of steel than he did.

Schwab says that he was paid this salary largely because of his ability to deal with people. I asked him how he did it. Here is his secret set down in his own words—words that ought to be cast in eternal bronze and hung in every home and school, every shop and office in the land; words that children ought to memorize instead of wasting their time memorizing the conjugation of Latin verbs or the amount of the annual rainfall in Brazil; words that will all but transform your life and mine if we will only live them:

"I consider my ability to arouse enthusiasm among my people," said Schwab, "the greatest asset I possess, and the way to develop the best that is in a person is by appreciation and encouragement.

"There is nothing else that so kills the ambitions of a person as criticisms from superiors. I never criticize anyone. I believe in giving a person incentive to work. So I am anxious to praise but loath to fault. If I like anything, I am hearty in my approbation and lavish in my praise."

That is what Schwab did. But what do average people do? The exact opposite. If they don't like a thing, they bawl out their subordinates; if they do like it, they say nothing. As the old couplet says: "Once I did bad and that I heard ever/Twice I did good, but that I heard never."

"In my wide association in life, meeting with many and great people in various parts of the world," Schwab declared, "I have yet to find the person, however great and exalted his station, who did not do better work and put forth greater effort under a spirit of approval than he would ever do under a spirit of criticism."

That, he said frankly, was one of the outstanding reasons for the phenomenal success of Andrew Carnegie. Carnegie praised his associates publicly as well as privately.

Carnegie wanted to praise his assistants even on his tombstone. He wrote an epitaph for himself that read: "Here lies one who knew how to get around him men who were cleverer than himself."

Sincere appreciation was one of the secrets of the first John D. Rockefeller's success in handling men. For example, when one of his partners, Edward T. Bedford, lost a million dollars for the firm by a bad buy in South America, John D. might have criticized; but he knew Bedford had done his best—and the incident was closed. So Rockefeller found something to praise; he congratulated Bedford because he had been able to save sixty percent of the money he had invested. "That's splendid," said Rockefeller. "We don't always do as well as that upstairs."

I have among my clippings a story that I know never happened, but it illustrates a truth, so I'll repeat it:

According to this silly story, a farm woman, at the end of a heavy day's work, set before her menfolks a heaping pile of hay. And when they indignantly demanded whether she had gone crazy, she replied: "Why, how did I know you'd notice? I've been cooking for you men for the last twenty years and in all that time I ain't heard no word to let me know you wasn't just eating hay."

When a study was made a few years ago on runaway wives, what do you think was discovered to be the main reasons wives ran away? It was "lack of appreciation." And I'd bet that a similar study made of runaway husbands would come out the same way. We often take our spouses so much for granted that we never let them know we appreciate them.

Florenz Ziegfeld, the most spectacular producer who ever dazzled Broadway, gained his reputation by his subtle ability to "glorify the American girl." Time after time, he took drab little creatures that no one ever looked at twice and transformed them on the stage into glamorous visions of mystery and seduction. Knowing the value of appreciation and confidence, he made women feel beautiful by the sheer power of his gallantry and consideration. He was practical: he raised the salary of chorus girls from $30 a week to as high as $175. And he was also chivalrous; on opening night at the Follies, he sent telegrams to the stars in the cast, and he deluged every chorus girl in the show with American Beauty roses.

I once succumbed to the fad of fasting and went for six days and nights without eating. It wasn't difficult. I was less hungry at the end of the sixth day than I was at the end of the second. Yet I know, as you know, people who would think they had committed a crime if they let their families or employees go for six days without food; but they will let them go for six days, and six weeks, and sometimes sixty years without giving them the hearty appreciation that they crave almost as much as they crave food.

When Alfred Lunt, one of the great actors of his time, played the leading role in *Reunion in Vienna*, he said, "There is nothing I need so much as nourishment for my self-esteem."

We nourish the bodies of our children and friends and employees, but how often do we nourish their self-esteem? We provide them with roast beef and potatoes to build energy, but we neglect to give them kind words of appreciation that would sing in their memories for years like the music of the morning stars.

Paul Harvey, in one of his radio broadcasts, "The Rest of the Story," told how showing sincere appreciation can change a persons life. He reported that years ago a teacher in Detroit asked Stevie Morris to help her find a mouse that was lost in the classroom. You see, she appreciated the fact that nature had given Stevie something no one else in the room had. Nature had given Stevie a remarkable pair of ears to compensate for his blind eyes. But this was really the first time Stevie had been shown appreciation for those talented ears. Now, years later, he says that this act of appreciation was the beginning of a new life. You see, from that time on he developed his gift of hearing and went on to become, under the stage name of Stevie Wonder, one of *the* great pop singers and songwriters of the seventies.

Some readers are saying right now as they read these lines; "Oh, phooey! Flattery! Bear oil! I've tried that stuff. It doesn't work—not with intelligent people."

Of course, flattery seldom works with discerning people. It is shallow, selfish, and insincere. It ought to fail and it usually does. True, some people are so hungry, so thirsty, for appreciation that they will swallow anything, just as a starving man will eat grass and fishworms.

Even Queen Victoria was susceptible to flattery. Prime Minister Benjamin Disraeli confessed that he laid it on thick in dealing with the queen. To use his exact words, he said he "spread it on with a trowel." But Disraeli was one of the most polished, deft, and adroit men who ever ruled the far-flung British Empire. He was a genius in his line. What would work for him wouldn't necessarily work for you and me. In the long run, flattery will do you more harm than good. Flattery is counterfeit, and like counterfeit money, it will eventually get you into trouble if you pass it to someone else.

The difference between appreciation and flattery? That is simple. One is sincere and the other insincere. One comes from the heart out; the other from the teeth out. One is unselfish; the other selfish. One is universally admired; the other universally condemned.

I recently saw a bust of the Mexican hero General Alvaro Obregon in the Chapultepec palace in Mexico City. Below the bust are carved these wise words from General Obregon's philosophy: "Don't be afraid of enemies who attack you. Be afraid of friends who flatter you."

No! No! No! I am not suggesting flattery? Far from it. I'm talking about a new way of life. Let me repeat. *I am talking about a new way of life.*

King George V had a set of six maxims displayed on the walls of his study at Buckingham Palace. One of these maxims said: "Teach me neither to proffer nor receive cheap praise." That's all flattery is—cheap praise. I once read a definition of flattery that may be worth repeating: "Flattery is telling the other person precisely what he thinks about himself."

"Use what language you will," said Ralph Waldo Emerson, "you can never say anything but what you are."

If all we had to do was flatter, everybody would catch on and we should all be experts in human relations.

When we are not engaged in thinking about some definite problem, we usually spend about ninety-five percent of our time thinking about ourselves. Now, if we stop thinking about ourselves for a while and begin to think of the other person's good points, we won't have to resort to flattery so cheap and false that it can be spotted almost before it is out of the mouth.

One of the most neglected virtues of our daily existence is appreciation. Somehow, we neglect to praise our son or daughter when he or she brings home a good report card, and we fail to encourage our children when they first succeed in baking a cake or building a birdhouse. Nothing pleases children more than this kind of parental interest and approval.

The next time you enjoy filet mignon at the club, send word to the chef that it was excellently prepared, and when a tired salesperson shows you unusual courtesy, please mention it.

Every minister, lecturer, and public speaker knows the discouragement of pouring himself or herself out to an audience and not receiving a single ripple of appreciative comment. What applies to professionals applies doubly to workers in offices, shops, and factories, and to our families and friends. In our interpersonal relations we should never forget that all our associates are human beings and hunger for appreciation. It is the legal tender that all souls enjoy.

Try leaving a friendly trail of little sparks of gratitude on your daily trips. You will be surprised how they will set small flames of friendship that will be rose beacons on your next visit.

Pamela Dunham of New Fairfield, Connecticut, had among her responsibilities on her job the supervision of a janitor who was doing a very poor job. The other employees would jeer at him and litter the hallways to show him what a bad job he was doing. It was so bad, productive time was being lost in the shop.

Without success, Pam tried various ways to motivate this person. She noticed that occasionally he did a particularly good piece of work. She made a point to praise him for it in front of the other people. Each day the job he did all around got better, and pretty soon he started doing all his work efficiently. Now he does an excellent job and other people give him appreciation and recognition. Honest appreciation got results where criticism and ridicule failed.

Hurting people not only does not change them, it is never called for. There is an old saying that I have cut out and pasted on my mirror, where I cannot help but see it every day:

> I shall pass this way but once; any good, therefore, that I can do or any kindness that I can show to any human being, let me do it now. Let me not defer nor neglect it, for I shall not pass this way again.

Emerson said: "Every man I meet is my superior in some way. In that, I learn of him."

If that was true of Emerson, isn't it likely to be a thousand times more true of you and me? Let's cease thinking of our accomplishments, our wants. Let's try to figure out the other person's good points. Then forget flattery. Give honest, sincere appreciation. Be "hearty in your approbation and lavish in your praise," and people will cherish your words and treasure them and repeat them over a lifetime—repeat them years after you have forgotten them.

One of the Most Neglected Virtues of Our Daily Existence is Appreciation.

4

"HE WHO CAN DO THIS HAS THE WHOLE WORLD WITH HIM. HE WHO CANNOT WALKS A LONELY WAY"

I often went fishing up in Maine during the summer. Personally I am very fond of strawberries and cream, but I have found that for some strange reason, fish prefer worms. So when I went fishing, I didn't think about what I wanted. I thought about what they wanted. I didn't bait the hook with strawberries and cream. Rather, I dangled a worm or a grasshopper in front of the fish and said: "Wouldn't you like to have that?"

Why not use the same common sense when fishing for people?

That is what Lloyd George, Great Britain's prime minister during World War I, did. When someone asked him how he managed to stay in power after the other wartime leaders—Wilson, Orlando, and Clemenceau— had been forgotten, he replied that if his staying on top might be attributed to any one thing, it would be to his having learned that it was necessary to bait the hook to suit the fish.

Why talk about what we want? That is childish. Absurd. Of course, you are interested in what you want. You are eternally interested in it. But no one else is. The rest of us are just like you: we are interested in what we want.

So the only way on earth to influence other people is to talk about what *they* want and show them how to get it.

Remember that tomorrow when you are trying to get somebody to do something. If, for example, you don't want your children to smoke, don't preach at them, and don't talk about what you want; but show them that cigarettes may keep them from making the basketball team or winning the hundred-yard dash.

This is a good thing to remember regardless of whether you are dealing with children or calves or chimpanzees. For example: One day Ralph Waldo Emerson and his son tried to get a calf into a barn. But they made the common mistake of thinking only of what they wanted. Emerson pushed and his son pulled. But the calf was doing just what they were doing: he was thinking only of what he wanted; so he stiffened his legs and stubbornly refused to leave the pasture. The Irish housemaid saw their predicament. She couldn't write essays and books; but, on this occasion at least, she had more horse sense, or calf sense, than Emerson had. She thought of what the calf wanted; so she put her maternal finger in the calf's mouth and let the calf suck her finger as she gently led him into the barn.

Every act you have performed since the day you were born was performed because you wanted something. How about the time you gave a large contribution to the Red Cross? Yes, that is no exception to the rule. You gave the Red Cross the donation because you wanted to lend a helping hand: you wanted to do a beautiful, unselfish, divine act. "Inasmuch as ye have done it unto the least of these my brethren, ye have done it unto me."

If you hadn't wanted that feeling more than you wanted your money, you would not have made the contribution. Of course, you might have made the contribution because you were ashamed to refuse or because a customer asked you to do it. But one thing is certain. You made the contribution because you wanted something.

Harry A. Overstreet in his illuminating book *Influencing Human Behavior* said: "Action springs out of what we fundamentally desire...and the best piece of advice which can be given to would-be persuaders, whether in business, in the home, in the school, in politics, is: First, arouse in the other person an eager want. He who can do this has the whole world with him. He who cannot walks a lonely way."

Andrew Carnegie, the poverty-stricken Scotch lad who started to work at two cents an hour and finally gave away $365 million, learned early in life that the only way to influence people is to talk in terms of what the other person wants. He attended school only four years; yet he learned how to handle people.

An example of persuading comes from Stan Novak of Cleveland, Ohio, a participant in our course. Stan came home from work one evening to find his youngest son, Tim, kicking and screaming on the living room floor. He was to start kindergarten the next day and was protesting that he would not go. Stan's normal reaction would have been to banish the child to his room and tell him he'd just better make up his mind to go. He had no choice. But tonight, recognizing that this would not really help Tim start kindergarten in the best frame of mind, Stan sat down and thought, "If I were Tim, why would I be excited about going to kindergarten?" He and his wife made a list of all the fun things Tim would do such as finger-painting, singing songs, making new friends. Then they put them into action. "We all started finger-painting on the kitchen table—my wife, Lil, my other son, Bob, and myself, all having fun. Soon Tim was peeping around the corner. Next he was begging to participate. 'Oh, no! You have to go to kindergarten first to learn how to finger- paint.' With all the enthusiasm I could muster I went through the list talking in terms he could understand— telling him all the fun he would have in kindergarten. The next morning, I thought I was the first one up. I went downstairs and found Tim sitting sound asleep in the living room chair. 'What are you doing here?' I asked. 'I'm waiting to go to kindergarten. I don't want to be late.' The enthusiasm of our entire family had aroused in Tim an eager want that no amount of discussion or threat could have possibly accomplished."

Tomorrow you may want to persuade somebody to do something. Before you speak, pause and ask yourself: "How can I make this person want to do it?"

That question will stop us from rushing into a situation heedlessly, with futile chatter about our desires.

At one time I rented the grand ballroom of a certain New York hotel for twenty nights in each season in order to hold a series of lectures.

At the beginning of one season, I was suddenly informed that I should have to pay almost three times as much rent as formerly. This news reached me after the tickets had been printed and distributed and all announcements had been made.

Naturally, I didn't want to pay the increase, but what was the use of talking to the hotel about what I wanted? They were interested only in what they wanted. So a couple of days later I went to see the manager.

"I was a bit shocked when I got your letter," I said, "but I don't blame you at all. If I had been in your position, I should probably have written a similar letter myself. Your duty as the manager of the hotel is to make all the profit possible. If you don't do that, you will be fired and you ought to be fired. Now, let's take a piece of paper and write down the advantages and the disadvantages that will accrue to you, if you insist on this increase in rent."

Then I took a letterhead and ran a line through the center and headed one column "Advantages" and the other column "Disadvantages."

I wrote down under the head "Advantages" these words: "Ballroom free." Then I went on to say: "You will have the advantages of having the ballroom free to rent for dances and conventions. That is a big advantage, for affairs like that will pay you much more than you can get for a series of lectures. If I tie your ballroom up for twenty nights during the course of the season, it is sure to mean a loss of some very profitable business to you.

"Now, let's consider the disadvantages. First, instead of increasing your income from me, you are going to decrease it. In fact, you are going to wipe it out because I cannot pay the rent you are asking. I shall be forced to hold these lectures at some other place.

"There's another disadvantage to you also. These lectures attract crowds of educated and cultured people to your hotel. That is good advertising for you, isn't it? In fact, if you spent five thousand dollars advertising in the newspapers, you couldn't bring as many people to look at your hotel as I can bring by these lectures. That is worth a lot to a hotel, isn't it?"

As I talked, I wrote these two "disadvantages" under the proper heading, and handed the sheet of paper to the manager, saying: "I wish you would carefully consider both the advantages and the disadvantages that are going to accrue to you and then give me your final decision."

I received a letter the next day, informing me that my rent would be increased only fifty percent instead of three hundred percent.

Mind you, I got this reduction without saying a word about what I wanted. I talked all the time about what the other person wanted and how he could get it.

Suppose I had done the human, natural thing; suppose I had stormed into his office and said, "What do you mean by raising my rent three hundred percent when you know the tickets have been printed and the announcements made? Three hundred percent! Ridiculous! Absurd! I won't pay it!"

What would have happened then? An argument would have begun to steam and boil and sputter—and you know how arguments end. Even if I had convinced him that he was wrong, his pride would have made it difficult for him to back down and give in.

Here is one of the best bits of advice ever given about the fine art of human relationships. "If there is any one secret of success," said Henry Ford, "it lies in the ability to get the other person's point of view and see things from that person's angle as well as from your own."

That is so good, I want to repeat it: "If there is any one secret of success, it lies in the ability to get the other person's point of view and see things from that person's angle as well as from your own."

That is so simple, so obvious, that anyone ought to see the truth of it at a glance; yet ninety percent of the people on this earth ignore it ninety percent of the time.

An example? Look at the letters that come across your desk tomorrow morning, and you will find that most of them violate this important canon of common sense. Take this one, a letter written by the head of the radio department of an advertising agency with offices scattered across the continent. This letter was sent to the managers of local radio stations throughout the country. (I have set down, in brackets, my reactions to each paragraph.)

Mr. John Blank,
Blankville,
Indiana

Dear Mr. Blank:

The company desires to retain its position in advertising agency leadership in the radio field.

[Who cares what your company desires? I am worried about my own problems. The bank is foreclosing the mortgage on my house, the bugs are destroying the hollyhocks, the stock market tumbled yesterday. I missed the eight-fifteen this morning, I wasn't invited to the Joneses' dance last night, the doctor tells me I have high blood pressure and neuritis and dandruff. And then what happens? I come down to the office this morning worried, open my mail, and here is some little whippersnapper off in New York yapping about what his company wants. Bah! If he only realized what sort of impression his letter makes, he would get out of the advertising business and start manufacturing sheep dip.]

This agency's national advertising accounts were the bulwark of the network. Our subsequent clearances of station time have kept us at the top of agencies year after year.

[You are big and rich and right at the top, aren't you? So what? I don't give two whoops in Hades if you are as big as General Motors and General Electric and the General Staff of the U.S. Army all combined. If you had as much sense as a half-witted hummingbird, you would realize that I am interested in how big I am—not how big you are. All this talk about your enormous success makes me feel small and unimportant.]

We desire to service our accounts with the last word on radio station information.

[You desire! You desire. You unmitigated ass. I'm not interested in what you desire or what the President of the United States desires. Let me tell you once and for all that I am interested in what I desire—and you haven't said a word about that yet in this absurd letter of yours.]

Will you, therefore, put the—company on your preferred list for weekly station information—every single detail that will be useful to an agency in intelligently booking time.

["Preferred list." You have your nerve! You make me feel insignificant by your big talk about your company— and then you ask me to put you on a "preferred" list, and you don't even say "please" when you ask it.]

A prompt acknowledgment of this letter, giving us your latest "doings," will be mutually helpful.

[You fool! You mail me a cheap form letter, a letter scattered far and wide like the autumn leaves, and you have the gall to ask me, when I am worried about the mortgage and the hollyhocks and my blood pressure, to sit down and dictate a personal note acknowledging your form letter—and you ask me to do it "promptly." What do you mean, "promptly"? Don't you know I am just as busy as you are—or, at least, I like to think I am. And while we are on the subject, who gave you the lordly right to order me around? You say it will be "mutually helpful." At last, at last, you have begun to see my viewpoint. But you are vague about how it will be to my advantage.]

Very truly yours,
John Doe
Manager, Radio Department

P.S. The enclosed reprint from the Blankville *Journal* will be of interest to you, and you may want to broadcast it over your station.

[Finally, down here in the postscript, you mention something that may help me solve one of my problems. Why didn't you begin your letter with—but what's the use? Any advertising man who is guilty of perpetrating such drivel as you have sent me has something wrong with his medulla oblongata. You don't need a letter giving our latest doings. What you need is a quart of iodine in your thyroid gland.]

Now, if people who devote their lives to advertising and who pose as experts in the art of influencing people to buy—if they write a letter like that, what can we expect from the butcher and baker or the auto mechanic?

Here is another letter, written by the superintendent of a large freight terminal to a student of this course, Edward Vermylen. What effect did this letter have on the man to whom it was addressed? Read it and then I'll tell you.

> A. Zerega's Sons, Inc.
> 28 Front Street
> Brooklyn, N.Y. 11201
> Attention: Mr. Edward Vermylen
>
> Gentlemen:
>
> The operations at our outbound-rail-receiving station are handicapped because a material percentage of the total business is delivered us in the late afternoon. This condition results in congestion, overtime on the part of our forces, delays to trucks, and in some cases delays to freight. On November 10, we received from your company a lot of 510 pieces, which reached here at 4:20 p.m.
>
> We solicit your cooperation toward overcoming the undesirable effects arising from late receipt of freight. May we ask that, on days on which you ship the volume which was received on the above date, effort be made either to get the truck here earlier or to deliver us part of the freight during the morning?
>
> The advantage that would accrue to you under such an arrangement would be that of more expeditious discharge of your trucks and the assurance that your business would go forward on the date of its receipt.
>
> Very truly yours,
> J— B—, Supt.

After reading this letter, Mr. Vermylen, sales manager for A. Zerega's Sons, Inc., sent it to me with the following comment:

> This letter had the reverse effect from that which was intended. The letter begins by describing the Terminal's difficulties, in which we are not interested, generally speaking. Our cooperation is then requested without any thought as to whether it would inconvenience us, and then, finally, in

the last paragraph, the fact is mentioned that if we do cooperate it will mean more expeditious discharge of our trucks with the assurance that our freight will go forward on the date of its receipt.

In other words, that in which we are most interested is mentioned last and the whole effect is one of raising a spirit of antagonism rather than of cooperation.

Let's see if we can't rewrite and improve this letter. Let's not waste any time talking about our problems. As Henry Ford admonishes, let's "get the other person's point of view and see things from his or her angle, as well as from our own."

Here is one way of revising the letter. It may not be the best way, but isn't it an improvement?

Mr. Edward Vermylen
c/o A. Zerega's Sons, Inc.
28 Front St.
Brooklyn, N.Y. 11201

Dear Mr. Vermylen:

Your company has been one of our good customers for fourteen years. Naturally, we are very grateful for your patronage and are eager to give you the speedy, efficient service you deserve. However, we regret to say that it isn't possible for us to do that when your trucks bring us a large shipment late in the afternoon, as they did on November 10. Why? Because many other customers make late-afternoon deliveries also. Naturally, that causes congestion. That means your trucks are held up unavoidably at the pier and sometimes even your freight is delayed.

That's bad, but it can be avoided. If you make your deliveries at the pier in the morning when possible, your trucks will be able to keep moving, your freight will get immediate attention, and our workers will get home early at night to enjoy a dinner of the delicious macaroni and noodles that you manufacture.

Regardless of when your shipments arrive, we shall always cheerfully do all in our power to serve you promptly.

You are busy. Please don't trouble to answer this note.

Very truly yours,
J—B—, Supt.

Barbara Anderson, who worked in a bank in New York, desired to move to Phoenix, Arizona, because of the health of her son. Using the principles she had learned in our course, she wrote the following letter to twelve banks in Phoenix:

> Dear Sir:
>
> My ten years of bank experience should be of interest to a rapidly growing bank like yours.
>
> In various capacities in bank operations with the Bankers Trust Company in New York, leading to my present assignment as branch manager, I have acquired skills in all phases of banking, including depositor relations, credits, loans, and administration.
>
> I will be relocating to Phoenix in May and I am sure I can contribute to your growth and profit. I will be in Phoenix the week of April 3 and would appreciate the opportunity to show you how I can help your bank meet its goals.
>
> Sincerely,
> Barbara L. Anderson

Do you think Mrs. Anderson received any response from that letter? Eleven of the twelve banks invited her to be interviewed, and she had a choice of which bank's offer to accept. Why? Mrs. Anderson did not state what *she* wanted, but wrote in the letter how she could help them, and focused on *their* wants, not her own.

Thousands of salespeople are pounding the pavements today, tired, discouraged, and underpaid. Why? Because they are always thinking only of what they want. They don't realize that neither you nor I want to buy anything. If we did, we would go out and buy it. But both of us are eternally interested in solving our problems. And if salespeople can show us how their services or merchandise will help us solve our problems, they won't need to sell us. We'll buy. And customers like to feel that they are buying—not being sold.

Yet many salespeople spend a lifetime in selling without seeing things from the customer's angle. For example, for many years I lived in Forest Hills, a little community of private homes in the center of

Greater New York. One day as I was rushing to the station, I chanced to meet a real-estate operator who had bought and sold property in that area for many years. He knew Forest Hills well, so I hurriedly asked him whether or not my stucco house was built with metal lath or hollow tile. He said he didn't know and told me what I already knew—that I could find out by calling the Forest Hills Garden Association. The following morning, I received a letter from him. Did he give me the information I wanted? He could have gotten it in sixty seconds by a telephone call. But he didn't. He told me again that I could get it by telephoning, and then asked me to let him handle my insurance.

He was not interested in helping me. He was interested only in helping himself.

J. Howard Lucas of Birmingham, Alabama, tells how two salespeople from the same company handled the same type of situation. He reported:

"Several years ago I was on the management team of a small company. Headquartered near us was the district office of a large insurance company. Their agents were assigned territories, and our company was assigned to two agents, who I shall refer to as Carl and John.

"One morning, Carl dropped by our office and casually mentioned that his company had just introduced a new life insurance policy for executives and thought we might be interested later on and he would get back to us when he had more information on it.

"The same day, John saw us on the sidewalk while returning from a coffee break, and he shouted: 'Hey, Luke, hold up, I have some great news for you fellows.' He hurried up and very excitedly told us about an executive life insurance policy his company had introduced that very day. (It was the same policy that Carl had casually mentioned.) He wanted us to have one of the first issued. He gave us a few important facts about the coverage and ended saying, 'The policy is so new, I'm going to have someone from the home office come out tomorrow and explain it. Now, in the meantime, let's get the applications signed and on the way so he can have more information to work with.' His enthusiasm aroused in us an eager want for this policy even though we still did not have details. When they were made available to us, they confirmed John's initial understanding of the policy, and he not only sold each of us a policy, but later doubled our coverage.

"Carl could have had those sales, but he made no effort to arouse in us any desire for the policies."

The world is full of people who are grabbing and self- seeking. So the rare individual who unselfishly tries to serve others has an enormous advantage. He has little competition. Owen D. Young, a noted lawyer and one of America's great business leaders, once said: "People who can put themselves in the place of other people, who can understand the workings of their minds, need never worry about what the future has in store for them."

If out of reading this book you get just one thing—an increased tendency to think always in terms of other people's point of view, and see things from their angle—if you get that one thing out of this book, it may easily prove to be one of the building blocks of your career.

Looking at the other person's point of view and arousing an eager want for something is not to be construed as manipulating that person to do something that is only for your benefit and his or her detriment. Each party should gain from the negotiation. In the letters to Mr. Vermylen, both the sender and the receiver of the correspondence gained by implementing what was suggested. Both the bank and Mrs. Anderson won by her letter in that the bank obtained a valuable employee and Mrs. Anderson a suitable job. And in the example of John's sale of insurance to Mr. Lucas, both gained through the transaction.

Another example in which everybody gains through this principle of arousing an eager want comes from Michael E. Whidden of Warwick, Rhode Island, who is a territory salesman for the Shell Oil Company. Mike wanted to become the number-one salesperson in his district, but one service station was holding back. It was run by an older man who could not be motivated to clean up his station. It was in such poor shape that sales were declining significantly.

The manager would not listen to any of Mike's pleas to upgrade the station. After many exhortations and heart- to-heart talks—all of which had no impact—Mike decided to invite the manager to visit the newest Shell station in his territory.

The manager was so impressed by the facilities at the new station that when Mike visited him the next time, his station was cleaned up and had recorded a sales increase. This enabled Mike to reach the number-one spot in his district. All his talking and discussion hadn't helped, but by arousing an eager want in the manager, by showing him the modern station, he had accomplished his goal, and both the manager and Mike benefited.

Most people go through college and learn to read Virgil and master the mysteries of calculus without ever discovering how their own minds function. For instance: I once gave a course in Effective Speaking for the young college graduates who were entering the employ of the Carrier Corporation, the large air-conditioner manufacturer. One of the participants wanted to persuade the others to play basketball in their free time, and this is about what he said: "I want you to come out and play basketball. I like to play basketball, but the last few times I've been to the gymnasium there haven't been enough people to get up a game. Two or three of us got to throwing the ball around the other night—and I got a black eye. I wish all of you would come down tomorrow night. I want to play basketball."

Did he talk about anything you want? You don't want to go to a gymnasium that no one else goes to, do you? You don't care about what he wants. You don't want to get a black eye.

Could he have shown you how to get the things you want by using the gymnasium? Surely. More pep. Keener edge to the appetite. Clearer brain. Fun. Games. Basketball.

To repeat Professor Overstreet's wise advice: First, arouse in the other person an eager want. He who can do this has the whole world with him. He who cannot walks a lonely way.

One of the students in the training course was worried about his little boy. The child was underweight and refused to eat properly. They scolded and nagged. "Mother wants you to eat this and that." "Father wants you to grow up to be a big man."

Did the boy pay any attention to these pleas? Just about as much as you would pay to one fleck of sand on a sandy beach.

No one with a trace of horse sense would expect a child three years old to react to the viewpoint of a father thirty years old. Yet that was precisely what that father had expected. It was absurd. He finally saw that. So he said to himself: "What does that boy want? How can I tie up what I want to what he wants?"

It was easy for the father when he started thinking about it. His boy had a tricycle that he loved to ride up and down the sidewalk in front of the house in Brooklyn. A few doors down the street lived a bully—a bigger boy who would pull the little boy off his tricycle and ride it himself.

Naturally, the little boy would run screaming to his mother, and she would have to come out and take the bully off the tricycle and put her little boy on again. This happened almost every day.

What did the little boy want? It didn't take a Sherlock Holmes to answer that one. His pride, his anger, his desire for a feeling of importance—all the strongest emotions in his makeup—goaded him to get revenge, to smash the bully in the nose. And when his father explained that the boy would be able to wallop the daylights out of the bigger kid someday if he would only eat the things his less hungry at the end of the sixth day than I was at the end of the second. Yet I know, as you know, people who would think they had committed a crime if they let their families or employees go for six days without food; but they will let them go for six days, and six weeks, and sometimes sixty years without giving them the hearty appreciation that they crave almost as much as they crave food.

When Alfred Lunt, one of the great actors of his time, played the leading role in *Reunion in Vienna*, he said, "There is nothing I need so much as nourishment for my self-esteem."

We nourish the bodies of our children and friends and employees, but how often do we nourish their self-esteem? We provide them with roast beef and potatoes to build energy, but we neglect to give them kind words of appreciation that would sing in their memories for years like the music of the morning stars.

Paul Harvey, in one of his radio broadcasts, "The Rest of the Story," told how showing sincere appreciation can change a person's life. He reported that years ago a teacher in Detroit asked Stevie Morris to help her find a mouse that was lost in the classroom. You see, she appreciated the fact that nature had given Stevie something no one else in the room had. Nature had given Stevie a remarkable pair of ears to compensate for his blind eyes. But this was really the first time Stevie had been shown appreciation for those talented ears. Now, years later, he says that this act of appreciation was the beginning of a new life. You see, from that time on he developed his gift of hearing and went on to become, under the stage name of Stevie Wonder, one of *the* great pop singers and songwriters of the seventies.

Some readers are saying right now as they read these lines; "Oh, phooey! Flattery! Bear oil! I've tried that stuff. It doesn't work—not with intelligent people."

Of course, flattery seldom works with discerning people. It is shallow, selfish, and insincere. It ought to fail and it usually does. True, some people are so hungry, so thirsty, for appreciation that they will swallow anything, just as a starving man will eat grass and fishworms.

Even Queen Victoria was susceptible to flattery. Prime Minister Benjamin Disraeli confessed that he laid it on thick in dealing with the queen. To use his exact words, he said he "spread it on with a trowel."

But Disraeli was one of the most polished, deft, and adroit men who ever ruled the far-flung British Empire. He was a genius in his line. What would work for him wouldn't necessarily work for you and me. In the long run, flattery will do you more harm than good. Flattery is counterfeit, and like counterfeit money, it will eventually get you into trouble if you pass it to someone else.

The difference between appreciation and flattery? That is simple. One is sincere and the other insincere. One comes from the heart out; the other from the teeth out. One is unselfish; the other selfish. One is universally admired; the other universally condemned.

I recently saw a bust of the Mexican hero General Alvaro Obregon in the Chapultepec palace in Mexico City. Below the bust are carved these wise words from General Obregon's philosophy: "Don't be afraid of enemies who attack you. Be afraid of friends who flatter you."

No! No! No! I am not suggesting flattery? Far from it. I'm talking about a new way of life. Let me repeat. *I am talking about a new way of life.*

King George V had a set of six maxims displayed on the walls of his study at Buckingham Palace. One of these maxims said: "Teach me neither to proffer nor receive cheap praise." That's all flattery is—cheap praise. I once read a definition of flattery that may be worth repeating: "Flattery is telling the other person precisely what he thinks about himself."

"Use what language you will," said Ralph Waldo Emerson, "you can never say anything but what you are."

If all we had to do was flatter, everybody would catch on and we should all be experts in human relations.

When we are not engaged in thinking about some definite problem, we usually spend about ninety-five percent of our time thinking about ourselves. Now, if we stop thinking about ourselves for a while and begin to think of the other person's good points, we won't have to resort to flattery so cheap and false that it can be spotted almost before it is out of the mouth.

One of the most neglected virtues of our daily existence is appreciation. Somehow, we neglect to praise our son or daughter when he or she brings home a good report card, and we fail to encourage our children when they first succeed in baking a cake or building a birdhouse. Nothing pleases children more than this kind of parental interest and approval.

The next time you enjoy filet mignon at the club, send word to the chef that it was excellently prepared, and when a tired salesperson shows you unusual courtesy, please mention it.

Every minister, lecturer, and public speaker knows the discouragement of pouring himself or herself out to an audience and not receiving a single ripple of appreciative comment. What applies to professionals applies doubly to workers in offices, shops, and factories, and to our families and friends. In our interpersonal relations we should never forget that all our associates are human beings and hunger for appreciation. It is the legal tender that all souls enjoy.

Try leaving a friendly trail of little sparks of gratitude on your daily trips. You will be surprised how they will set small flames of friendship that will be rose beacons on your next visit.

Pamela Dunham of New Fairfield, Connecticut, had among her responsibilities on her job the supervision of a janitor who was doing a very poor job. The other employees would jeer at him and litter the hallways to show him what a bad job he was doing. It was so bad, productive time was being lost in the shop.

Without success, Pam tried various ways to motivate this person. She noticed that occasionally he did a particularly good piece of work. She made a point to praise him for it in front of the other people. Each day the job he did all around got better, and pretty soon he started doing all his work efficiently. Now he does an excellent job and other people give him appreciation and recognition. Honest appreciation got results where criticism and ridicule failed.

Hurting people not only does not change them, it is never called for. There is an old saying that I have cut out and pasted on my mirror, where I cannot help but see it every day:

> I shall pass this way but once; any good, therefore, that I can do or any kindness that I can show to any human being, let me do it now Let me not defer nor neglect it, for I shall not pass this way again.

Emerson said: "Every man I meet is my superior in some way. In that, I learn of him."

If that was true of Emerson, isn't it likely to be a thousand times more true of you and me? Let's cease thinking of our accomplishments, our wants. Let's try to figure out the other person's good points. Then forget flattery. Give honest, sincere appreciation. Be "hearty in your approbation and lavish in your praise," and people will cherish your words and treasure them and repeat them over a lifetime—repeat them years after you have forgotten them.

One of the Most Neglected Virtues of Our Daily Existence is Appreciation.

5

HOW TO GET COOPERATION

Don't you have much more faith in ideas that you discover for yourself than in ideas that are handed to you on a silver platter? If so, isn't it bad judgment to try to ram your opinions down the throats of other people? Isn't it wiser to make suggestions—and let the other person think out the conclusion?

Adolph Seltz of Philadelphia, sales manager in an automobile showroom and a student in one of my courses, suddenly found himself confronted with the necessity of injecting enthusiasm into a discouraged and disorganized group of automobile salespeople. Calling a sales meeting, he urged his people to tell him exactly what they expected from him. As they talked, he wrote their ideas on the blackboard. He then said: "I'll give you all these qualities you expect from me. Now I want you to tell me what I have a right to expect from you." The replies came quick and fast: loyalty, honesty, initiative, optimism, teamwork, eight hours a day of enthusiastic work. The meeting ended with a new courage, a new inspiration—one salesperson volunteered to work fourteen hours a day—and Mr. Seltz reported to me that the increase of sales was phenomenal.

"The people had made a sort of moral bargain with me," said Mr. Seltz, "and as long as I lived up to my part in it, they were determined to live up to theirs. Consulting them about their wishes and desires was just the shot in the arm they needed."

No one likes to feel that he or she is being sold something or told to do a thing. We much prefer to feel that we are buying of our own accord or acting on our own ideas. We like to be consulted about our wishes, our wants, our thoughts.

Take the case of Eugene Wesson. He lost countless thousands of dollars in commissions before he learned this truth. Mr. Wesson sold sketches for a studio that created designs for stylists and textile manufacturers. Mr. Wesson had called on one of the leading stylists in New York once a week, every week for three years. “He never refused to see me,” said Mr. Wesson, “but he never bought. He always looked over my sketches very carefully and then said: ‘No, Wesson, I guess we don’t get together today.’”

After 150 failures, Wesson realized he must be in a mental rut, so he resolved to devote one evening a week to the study of influencing human behavior, to help him develop new ideas and generate new enthusiasm.

He decided on this new approach. With half a dozen unfinished artists’ sketches under his arm, he rushed over to the buyer’s office. “I want you to do me a little favor, if you will,” he said. “Here are some uncompleted sketches. Won’t you please tell me how we could finish them up in such a way that you could use them?”

The buyer looked at the sketches for a while without uttering a word. Finally he said: “Leave these with me for a few days, Wesson, and then come back and see me.”

Wesson returned three days later, got his suggestions, took the sketches back to the studio, and had them finished according to the buyer’s ideas. The result? All accepted.

After that, this buyer ordered scores of other sketches from Wesson, all drawn according to the buyer’s ideas. “I realized why I had failed for years to sell him,” said Mr. Wesson. “I had urged him to buy what I thought he ought to have. Then I changed my approach completely. I urged him to give me his ideas. This made him feel that he was creating the designs. And he was. I didn’t have to sell him. He bought.”

Letting the other person feel that the idea is his or hers not only works in business and politics, it works in family life as well. Paul M. Davis of Tulsa, Oklahoma, told his class how he applied this principle:

"My family and I enjoyed one of the most interesting sightseeing vacation trips we have ever taken. I had long dreamed of visiting such historic sites as the Civil War battlefield in Gettysburg, Independence Hall in Philadelphia, and our nation's capital. Valley Forge, Jamestown, and the restored colonial village of Williamsburg were high on the list of things I wanted to see.

"In March my wife, Nancy, mentioned that she had ideas for our summer vacation which included a tour of the western states, visiting points of interest in New Mexico, Arizona, California, and Nevada. She had wanted to make this trip for several years. But we couldn't, obviously, make both trips.

"Our daughter, Anne, had just completed a course in U.S. history in junior high school and had become very interested in the events that shaped our country's growth. I asked her how she would like to visit the places she had learned about on our next vacation. She said she would love to.

"Two evenings later as we sat around the dinner table, Nancy announced that if we all agreed, the summer's vacation would be to the eastern states, that it would be a great trip for Anne and thrilling for all of us. We all concurred."

This same psychology was used by an X-ray manufacturer to sell his equipment to one of the largest hospitals in Brooklyn. This hospital was building an addition and preparing to equip it with the finest X-ray department in America. Dr. L—, who was in charge of the X-ray department, was overwhelmed with sales representatives, each caroling the praises of his own company's equipment.

One manufacturer, however, was more skillful. He knew far more about handling human nature than the others did. He wrote a letter something like this:

> Our factory has recently completed a new line of X-ray equipment. The first shipment of these machines has just arrived at our office. They are not perfect. We know that, and we want to improve them. So we should be deeply obligated to you if you could find time to look them over and give us your ideas about how they can be made more serviceable to your profession. Knowing how occupied you are, I shall be glad to send my car for you at any hour you specify.

"I was surprised to get that letter," Dr. L—said as he related the incident before the class. "I was both surprised and complimented. I had never had an X-ray manufacturer seeking my advice before. It made me feel important. I was busy every night that week, but I canceled a dinner appointment in order to look over the equipment. The more I studied it, the more I discovered for myself how much I liked it.

"Nobody had tried to sell it to me. I felt that the idea of buying that equipment for the hospital was my own. I sold myself on its superior qualities and ordered it installed."

Ralph Waldo Emerson in his essay "Self-Reliance" stated: "In every work of genius we recognize our own rejected thoughts; they come back to us with a certain alienated majesty."

Colonel Edward M. House wielded an enormous influence in national and international affairs while Woodrow Wilson occupied the White House. Wilson leaned upon Colonel House for secret counsel and advice more than he did upon even members of his own cabinet.

What method did the colonel use in influencing the President? Fortunately, we know, for House himself revealed it to Arthur D. Howden Smith, and Smith quoted House in an article in *The Saturday Evening Post.*

"After I got to know the President,' House said, 'I learned the best way to convert him to an idea was to plant it in his mind casually, but so as to interest him in it—so as to get him thinking about it on his own account. The first time this worked it was an accident. I had been visiting him at the White House and urged a policy on him which he appeared to disapprove. But several days later, at the dinner table, I was amazed to hear him trot out my suggestion as his own.'"

Did House interrupt him and say, "That's not your idea. That's mine"? Oh, no. Not House. He was too adroit for that. He didn't care about credit. He wanted results. So he let Wilson continue to feel that the idea was his. House did even more than that. He gave Wilson public credit for these ideas.

Let's remember that everyone we come in contact with is just as human as Woodrow Wilson. So let's use Colonel House's technique.

A man up in the beautiful Canadian province of New Brunswick used this technique on me and won my patronage. I was planning at the time to do some fishing and canoeing in New Brunswick. So I wrote the tourist bureau for information. Evidently my name and address were put on a mailing list, for I was immediately overwhelmed with scores of letters and booklets and printed testimonials from camps and guides. I was bewildered. I didn't know which to choose. Then one camp owner did a clever thing. He sent me the names and telephone numbers of several New York people who had stayed at his camp and he invited me to telephone them and discover for myself what he had to offer.

I found to my surprise that I knew one of the men on his list. I telephoned him, found out what his experience had been, and then wired the camp the date of my arrival.

The others had been trying to sell me their service, but one let me sell myself. That organization won.

Twenty-five centuries ago, Lao-tse, a Chinese sage, said some things that readers of this book might use today:

"The reason why rivers and seas receive the homage of a hundred mountain streams is that they keep below them. Thus they are able to reign over all the mountain streams. So the sage, wishing to be above men, putteth himself below them; wishing to be before them, he putteth himself behind them. Thus, though his place be above men, they do not feel his weight; though his place be before them, they do not count it an injury."

Let the Other Person Feel that the Idea is His or Hers

* * *

Men of age object too much, consult too long, adventure too little, repent too soon, and seldom drive business home to the full period, but content themselves with a mediocrity of success.

– Dale Carnegie

6

AN APPEAL THAT EVERYBODY LIKES

I was reared on the edge of the Jesse James country out in Missouri, and I visited the James farm at Kearney, Missouri, where the son of Jesse James was then living.

His wife told me stories of how Jesse robbed trains and held up banks and. then gave money to the neighboring farmers to pay off their mortgages.

Jesse James probably regarded himself as an idealist at heart, just as Dutch Schultz, "Two Gun" Crowley, Al Capone, and many other organized crime "godfathers" did generations later. The fact is that all people you meet have a high regard for themselves and like to be fine and unselfish in their own estimation.

J. Pierpont Morgan observed, in one of his analytical interludes, that a person usually has two good reasons for doing a thing: one that sounds good and a real one. The person himself will think of the real reason. You don't need to emphasize that. But all of us, being idealists at heart, like to think of motives that sound good. So, in order to change people, appeal to the nobler motives.

Is that too idealistic to work in business? Let's see. Let's take the case of Hamilton J. Farrell of the Farrell-Mitchell Company of Glenolden, Pennsylvania. Mr. Farrell had a disgruntled tenant who threatened to move. The tenant's lease still had four months to run; nevertheless, he served notice that he was vacating immediately, regardless of lease.

"These people had lived in my house all winter—the most expensive part of the year," Mr. Farrell said as he told the story to the class, "and I knew it would be difficult to rent the apartment again before fall. I could see all that rent income going over the hill and believe me, I saw red.

"Now, ordinarily, I would have waded into that tenant and advised him to read his lease again. I would have pointed out that if he moved, the full balance of his rent would fall due at once—and that I could, *and would*, take steps to collect.

"However, instead of flying off the handle and making a scene, I decided to try other tactics. So I started like this: 'Mr. Doe,' I said, 'I have listened to your story, and I still don't believe you intend to move. Years in the renting business have taught me something about human nature, and I sized you up in the first place as being a man of your word. In fact, I'm so sure of it that I'm willing to take a gamble.

"'Now, here's my proposition. Lay your decision on the table for a few days and think it over. If you come back to me between now and the first of the month, when the rent is due, and tell me you still intend to move, I give you my word I will accept your decision as final. I will give you the privilege of moving and admit to myself I've been wrong in my judgment. But I still believe you're a man of your word and will live up to your contract. For after all, we are either men or monkeys—and the choice usually lies with ourselves!'

"Well, when the new month came around, this gentleman came to see me and paid his rent in person. He and his wife had talked it over, he said—and decided to stay. They had concluded that the only honorable thing to do was to live up to their lease."

When the late Lord Northcliffe found a newspaper using a picture of him which he didn't want published, he wrote the editor a letter. But did he say, "Please do not publish that picture of me anymore; I don't like it"? No, he appealed to a nobler motive. He appealed to the respect and love that all of us have for motherhood. He wrote, "Please do not publish that picture of me anymore. My mother doesn't like it."

When John D. Rockefeller, Jr., wished to stop newspaper photographers from snapping pictures of his children, he, too, appealed to the nobler motives. He didn't say: "I don't want the pictures published." No, he appealed to the desire, deep in all of us, to refrain from harming children. He said: "You know how it is, boys. You've got children yourselves, some of you. And you know it's not good for youngsters to get too much publicity."

When Cyrus H. K. Curtis, a poor boy from Maine, was starting on the meteoric career which was destined to make him millions as owner of *The Saturday Evening Post* and the *Ladies Home Journal*, he couldn't afford to pay his contributors the prices that other magazines paid. He couldn't afford to hire first-class authors to write for money alone. So he appealed to their nobler motives. For example, he persuaded even Louisa May Alcott, the immortal author of *Little Women*, to write for him when she was at the flood tide of her fame; and he did it by offering to send a check for a hundred dollars, not to her, but to her favorite charity.

Right here the skeptic may say: "Oh, that stuff is all right for Northcliffe and Rockefeller or a sentimental novelist. But I'd like to see you make it work with the tough babies I have to collect bills from!"

You may be right. Nothing will work in all cases—and nothing will work with all people. If you are satisfied with the results you are getting, why change? If you are not satisfied, why not experiment?

At any rate, I think you will enjoy reading this true story told by James L. Thomas, a former student of mine:

Six customers of a certain automobile company refused to pay their bills for servicing. None of the customers protested the entire bill, but each claimed that some one charge was wrong. In each case, the customer had signed for the work done, so the company knew it was right— and said so. That was the first mistake.

Here are the steps the credit department took to collect these overdue bills. Do you suppose they succeeded?

They called on the customers and told them bluntly that they had come to collect a bill that was long past due.

They made it very plain that the company was absolutely and unconditionally right; therefore, the customer was absolutely and unconditionally wrong.

They intimated that they, the company, knew more about automobiles than the customer could ever hope to know. So what was the argument about?

Result: They argued.

Did any of these methods reconcile the customer and settle the account? You can answer that one yourself.

At this stage of affairs, the credit manager was about to open fire with a battery of legal talent, when fortunately the matter came to the attention of the general manager. The manager investigated these defaulting clients and discovered that they all had the reputation of paying their bills promptly. Something was wrong here—something was drastically wrong about the method of collection. So he called in James L. Thomas and told him to collect these "uncollectible" accounts.

Here, in his words, are the steps Mr. Thomas took:

"My visit to each customer was likewise to collect a bill long past due—a bill that we knew was absolutely right. But I didn't say a word about that. I explained I had called to find out what it was the company had done, or failed to do.

"I made it clear that, until I heard the customer's story, I had no opinion to offer. I told him the company made no claims to being infallible.

"I told him I was interested only in his car, and that he knew more about his car than anyone else in the world; that he was the authority on the subject.

"I let him talk, and I listened to him with all the interest and sympathy that he wanted—and expected.

"Finally, when the customer was in a reasonable mood, I put the whole thing up to his sense of fair play. I appealed to the nobler motives.

'First,' I said, 'I want you to know I also feel this matter has been badly mishandled. You've been inconvenienced and annoyed and irritated by one of our representatives. That should never have happened. I'm sorry and, as a representative of the company, I apologize. As I sat here and listened to your side of the story, I could not help being impressed by your fairness and patience. And now, because you are fair-minded and patient, I am going to ask you do to something for me. It's something that you can do better than anyone else, something you know more about than anyone else. Here is your bill; I know it is safe for me to adjust it, just as you would do if you were the president of my company. I am going to leave it all up to you. Whatever you say goes.'

"Did he adjust the bill? He certainly did, and got quite a kick out of it. The bills ranged from $ 150 to $400—but did the customer give himself the best of it? Yes, one of them did! One of them refused to pay a penny of the disputed charge; but the other five all gave the company the best of it! And here's the cream of the whole thing: we delivered new cars to all six of these customers within the next two years!"

"Experience has taught me," says Mr. Thomas, "that when no information can be secured about the customer the only sound basis on which to proceed is to assume that he or she is sincere, honest, truthful, and willing and anxious to pay the charges, once convinced they are correct. To put it differently and perhaps more clearly, people are honest and want to discharge their obligations. The exceptions to that rule are comparatively few, and I am convinced that the individuals who are inclined to chisel will in most cases react favorably if you make them feel that you consider them honest, upright, and fair."

In Order to Change People, Appeal to the Nobler Motives

* * *

Most of the important things in the world have been accomplished by people who have kept on trying when there seemed to be no hope at all.

– Dale Carnegie

7

A SURE WAY OF MAKING ENEMIES AND HOW TO AVOID IT

When Theodore Roosevelt was in the White House, he confessed that if he could be right seventy-five percent of the time, he would reach the highest measure of his expectation.

If that was the highest rating that one of the most distinguished men of the twentieth century could hope to obtain, what about you and me?

If you can be sure of being right only fifty-five percent of the time, you can go down to Wall Street and make a million dollars a day. If you can't be sure of being right even fifty-five percent of the time, why should you tell other people they are wrong?

You can tell people they are wrong by a look or an intonation or a gesture just as eloquently as you can in words—and if you tell them they are wrong, do you make them want to agree with you? Never! For you have *Struck* a direct blow at their intelligence, judgment, pride, and self-respect. That will make them want to strike back. But it will never make them want to change their minds. You may then hurl at them all the logic of a Plato or an Immanuel Kant, but you will not alter their opinions, for you have hurt their feelings.

Never begin by announcing, "I am going to prove so- and-so to you." That's bad. That's tantamount to saying: "I'm smarter than you are. I'm going to tell you a thing or two and make you change your mind."

That is a challenge. It arouses opposition and makes the listener want to battle with you before you even start. It is difficult, under even the most benign conditions, to change people's minds. So why make it harder? Why handicap yourself?

Well, I can't hope to be any smarter than Socrates, so I have quit telling people they are wrong. And I find that it pays.

If a person makes a statement that you think is wrong—yes, even that you know is wrong—isn't it better to begin by saying: "Well, now, look. I thought otherwise, but I may be wrong. I frequently am. And if I am wrong, I want to be put right. Let's examine the facts."

There's magic, positive magic, in such phrases as: "I may be wrong. I frequently am. Let's examine the facts."

Nobody in the heavens above or on the earth will ever object to your saying: "I may be wrong. Let's examine the facts."

One of our class members who used this approach in dealing with customers was Harold Reinke, a Dodge dealer in Billings, Montana. He reported that because of the pressures of the automobile business, he was often hard-boiled and callous when dealing with customers complaints. This caused flared tempers, loss of business, and general unpleasantness.

He told his class: "Recognizing that this was getting me nowhere fast, I tried a new tack. I would say something like this: 'Our dealership has made so many mistakes that I am frequently ashamed. We have erred in your case. Tell me about it.'

"This approach becomes quite disarming, and by the time the customer releases his feelings, he is usually much more reasonable when it comes to settling the matter. In fact, several customers have thanked me for having such an understanding attitude. And two of them have even brought in friends to buy new cars. In this highly competitive market, we need more of this type of customer, and I believe that showing respect for all customers opinions and treating them diplomatically and courteously will help beat the competition."

You will never get into trouble by admitting that you may be wrong. That will stop all argument and inspire your opponent to be just as fair and open and broad- minded as you are. It will make him want to admit that he, too, may be wrong.

If you know positively that a person is wrong, and you bluntly tell him or her so, what happens? Let me illustrate. Mr. S, a young New York attorney, once argued a rather important case before the United States Supreme Court (Lustgarten v. Fleet Corporation 280 U.S. 320). The case involved a considerable sum of money and an important question of law. During the argument, one of the Supreme Court justices said to him: "The statute of limitations is six years, is it not?"

Mr. S stopped, stared at the justice for a moment, and then said bluntly, "Your Honor, there is no statute of limitations in admiralty."

"A hush fell on the court," said Mr. S, as he related his experience to one of the author's classes, "and the temperature in the room seemed to drop to zero. I was right. Justice was wrong. And I had told him so. But did that make him friendly? No. I still believe that I had the law on my side. And I know that I spoke better than I ever spoke before. But I didn't persuade. I made the enormous blunder of telling a very learned and famous man that he was wrong."

Few people are logical. Most of us are prejudiced and biased. Most of us are blighted with preconceived notions, with jealousy, suspicion, fear, envy, and pride. And most citizens don't want to change their minds about their religion or their haircut or communism or their favorite movie star.

Carl Rogers, the eminent psychologist, wrote in his book *On Becoming a Person:*

> I have found it of enormous value when I can permit myself to understand the other person. The way in which I have worded this statement may seem strange to you. Is it necessary to permit oneself to understand another? I think it is. Our first reaction to most of the statements [which we hear from other people] is an evaluation or judgment, rather than an understanding of it. When someone expresses some feeling, attitude or belief, our tendency

> is almost immediately to feel "that's right," or "that's stupid," "that's abnormal," "that's unreasonable," "that's incorrect," "that's not nice." Very rarely do we permit ourselves to *understand* precisely what the meaning of the statement is to the other person.

I once employed an interior decorator to make some draperies for my home. When the bill arrived, I was dismayed.

A few days later, a friend dropped in and looked at the draperies. The price was mentioned, and she exclaimed with a note of triumph: "What? That's awful. I am afraid he put one over on you."

True? Yes, she had told the truth, but few people like to listen to truths that reflect on their judgment. So, being human, I tried to defend myself. I pointed out that the best is eventually the cheapest, that one can't expect to get quality and artistic taste at bargain-basement prices, and so on and on.

The next day another friend dropped in, admired the draperies, bubbled over with enthusiasm, and expressed a wish that she could afford such exquisite creations for her home. My reaction was totally different. "Well, to tell the truth," I said, "I can't afford them myself. I paid too much. I'm sorry I ordered them."

When we are wrong, we may admit it to ourselves. And if we are handled gently and tactfully, we may admit it to others and even take pride in our frankness and broad-mindedness. But not if someone else is trying to ram the unpalatable fact down our esophagus.

Horace Greeley, the most famous editor in America during the time of the Civil War, disagreed violently with Lincoln's policies. He believed that he could drive Lincoln into agreeing with him by a campaign of argument, ridicule, and abuse. He waged this bitter campaign month after month, year after year. In fact, he wrote a brutal, bitter, sarcastic, and personal attack on President Lincoln the night Booth shot him.

But did all this bitterness make Lincoln agree with Greeley? Not at all. Ridicule and abuse never do.

If you want some excellent suggestions about dealing with people and managing yourself and improving your personality, read Benjamin Franklin's autobiography— one of the most fascinating life stories ever written, one of the classics of American literature. Ben Franklin tells how he conquered the iniquitous habit of argument and transformed himself into one of the most able, suave, and diplomatic men in American history.

One day, when Ben Franklin was a blundering youth, an old Quaker friend took him aside and lashed him with a few stinging truths, something like this:

> Ben, you are impossible. Your opinions have a slap in them for everyone who differs with you. They have become so offensive that nobody cares for them. Your friends find they enjoy themselves better when you are not around. You know so much that no man can tell you anything. Indeed, no man is going to try, for the effort would lead only to discomfort and hard work. So you are not likely ever to know any more than you do now, which is very little.

One of the finest things I know about Ben Franklin is the way he accepted that smarting rebuke. He was big enough and wise enough to realize that it was true, to sense that he was headed for failure and social disaster. So he made a right-about-face. He began immediately to change his insolent, opinionated ways.

"I made it a rule," said Franklin, "to forbear all direct contradiction to the sentiment of others, and all positive assertion of my own. I even forbade myself the use of every word or expression in the language that imported a fix'd opinion, such as 'certainly,' 'undoubtedly,' etc., and I adopted, instead of them, 'I conceive,' 'I apprehend,' or 'I imagine' a thing to be so or so, or 'it so appears to me at present.' When another asserted something that I thought an error, I deny'd myself the pleasure of contradicting him abruptly, and of showing immediately some absurdity in his proposition: and in answering I began by observing that in certain cases or instances his opinion would be right, but in the present case there appear'd or seem'd to me some difference, etc. I soon found the advantage of this change in my manner; the conversations I engag'd in went on more pleasantly. The modest way in which I propos'd my opinions procur'd them a readier reception and less contradiction; I had less mortification when I was found to be in the wrong, and I more easily prevail'd with others to give up their mistakes and join with me when I happened to be in the right.

"And this mode, which I at first put on with some violence to natural inclination, became at length so easy, and so habitual to me, that perhaps for these fifty years past no one has ever heard a dogmatical expression escape me. And to this habit (after my character of integrity) I think it principally owing that I had earned so much weight with my fellow citizens when I proposed new institutions, or alterations in the old, and so much influence in public councils when I became a member; for I was but a bad speaker, never eloquent, subject to much hesitation in my choice of words, hardly correct in language, and yet I generally carried my points."

How do Ben Franklin's methods work in business? Let's take two examples.

Katherine A. Allred of Kings Mountain, North Carolina, is an industrial engineering supervisor for a yarn-processing plant. She told one of our classes how she handled a sensitive problem before and after taking our training:

"Part of my responsibility," she reported, "deals with setting up and maintaining incentive systems and standards for our operators so they can make more money by producing more yarn. The system we were using had worked fine when we had only two or three different types of yarn, but recently we had expanded our inventory and capabilities to enable us to run more than twelve different varieties. The present system was no longer adequate to pay the operators fairly for the work being performed and give them an incentive to increase production. I had worked up a new system which would enable us to pay the operator by the class of yarn she was running at any one particular time. With my new system in hand, I entered the meeting determined to prove to the management that my system was the right approach. I told them in detail how they were wrong and showed where they were being unfair and how I had all the answers they needed. To say the least, I failed miserably! I had become so busy defending my position on the new system that I had left them no opening to graciously admit their problems on the old one. The issue was dead.

"After several sessions of this course, I realized all too well where I had made my mistakes. I called another meeting and this time I asked where they felt their problems were. We discussed each point, and I asked them their opinions on which was the best way to proceed. With a few low-keyed suggestions, at proper intervals, I let them develop my system themselves. At the end of the meeting when I actually presented my system, they enthusiastically accepted it.

"I am convinced now that nothing good is accomplished and a lot of damage can be done if you tell a person straight out that he or she is wrong. You only succeed in stripping that person of self-dignity and making yourself an unwelcome part of any discussion."

Let's take another example—and remember these cases I am citing are typical of the experiences of thousands of other people. R. V. Crowley was a salesman for a lumber company in New York. Crowley admitted that he had been telling hard-boiled lumber inspectors for years that they were wrong. And he had won the arguments too. I But it hadn't done any good. "For these lumber inspectors," said Mr. Crowley, "are like baseball umpires. Once they make a decision, they never change it."

Mr. Crowley saw that his firm was losing thousands of dollars through the arguments he won. So while taking my course, he resolved to change tactics and abandon arguments. With what results? Here is the story as he told it to the fellow members of his class:

"One morning the phone rang in my office. A hot and bothered person at the other end proceeded to inform me that a car of lumber we had shipped into his plant was entirely unsatisfactory. His firm had stopped unloading and requested that we make immediate arrangements to remove the stock from their yard. After about one-fourth of the car had been unloaded, their lumber inspector reported that the lumber was running fifty-five percent below grade. Under the circumstances, they refused to accept it.

"I immediately started for his plant and on the way turned over in my mind the best way to handle the situation. Ordinarily, under such circumstances, I should have quoted grading rules and tried, as a result of my own experience and knowledge as a lumber inspector, to convince the other inspector that the lumber was actually up to grade, and that he was misinterpreting the rules in his inspection. However, I thought I would apply the principles learned in this training.

"When I arrived at the plant, I found the purchasing agent and the lumber inspector in a wicked humor, both set for an argument and a fight. We walked out to the car that was being unloaded, and I requested that they continue to unload so that I could see how things were going. I asked the inspector to go right ahead and lay out the rejects, as he had been doing, and to put the good pieces in another pile.

"After watching him for a while it began to dawn on me that his inspection actually was much too strict and that he was misinterpreting the rules. This particular lumber was white pine, and I knew the inspector was thoroughly schooled in hard woods but not a competent, experienced inspector on white pine. White pine happened to be my own strong suit, but did I offer any objection to the way he was grading the lumber? None whatever. I kept on watching and gradually began to ask questions as to why certain pieces were not satisfactory. I didn't for one instant insinuate that the inspector was wrong. I emphasized that my only reason for asking was in order that we could give his firm exactly what they wanted in future shipments.

"By asking questions in a very friendly, cooperative spirit, and insisting continually that they were right in laying out boards not satisfactory to their purpose, I got him warmed up, and the strained relations between us began to thaw and melt away. An occasional carefully put remark on my part gave birth to the idea in his mind that possibly some of these rejected pieces were actually within the grade that they had bought, and that their requirements demanded a more expensive grade. I was very careful, however, not to let him think I was making an issue of this point.

"Gradually his whole attitude changed. He finally admitted to me that he was not experienced on white pine and began to ask me questions about each piece as it came out of the car. I would explain why such a piece came within the grade specified, but kept on insisting that we did not want him to take it if it was unsuitable for their purpose. He finally got to the point where he felt guilty every time he put a piece in the rejected pile. And at last he saw that the mistake was on their part for not having specified as good a grade as they needed.

"The ultimate outcome was that he went through the entire carload again after I left, accepted the whole lot, and we received a check in full.

"In that one instance alone, a little tact, and the determination to refrain from telling the other man he was wrong, saved my company a substantial amount of cash, and it would be hard to place a money value on the good will that was saved."

Martin Luther King, Jr., was asked how, as a pacifist, he could be an admirer of Air Force General Daniel "Chappie" James, then the nation's highest-ranking black officer. Dr. King replied, "I judge people by their own principles—not by my own."

In a similar way, General Robert E. Lee once spoke to the president of the Confederacy, Jefferson Davis in the most glowing terms about a certain officer under his command. Another officer was astonished. "General," he said, "do you not know that the man of whom you speak so highly is one of your bitterest enemies who misses no opportunity to malign you?" "Yes," replied General Lee, "but the president asked my opinion of him; he did not ask for his opinion of me."

By the way, I am not revealing anything new in this chapter. Two thousand years ago, Jesus said: "Agree with thine adversary quickly."

And twenty-two hundred years before Christ was born, Pharaoh Akhtoi of Egypt gave his son some shrewd advice—advice that is sorely needed today. "Be diplomatic," counseled the pharaoh. "It will help you gain your point."

In other words, don't argue with your customer or your spouse or your adversary. Don't tell them they are wrong, don't get them stirred up. Use a little diplomacy.

Be Diplomatic

* * *

Most of us have far more courage than we ever dreamed possible.

– Dale Carnegie

8

HOW TO CRITICIZE AND NOT BE HATED FOR IT

Charles Schwab was passing through one of his steel mills one day at noon when he came across some of his employees smoking. Immediately above their heads was a sign that said No Smoking. Did Schwab point to the sign and say, "Can't you read?" Oh, no, not Schwab. He walked over to the men, handed each one a cigar, and said, "I'll appreciate it, boys, if you will smoke these on the outside." They knew that he knew that they had broken a rule—and they admired him because he said nothing about it and gave them a little present and made them feel important. Couldn't keep from loving a man like that, could you?

John Wanamaker used the same technique. Wanamaker used to make a tour of his great store in Philadelphia every day. Once he saw a customer waiting at a counter. No one was paying the slightest attention to her. The salespeople? Oh, they were in a huddle at the far end of the counter laughing and talking among themselves. Wanamaker didn't say a word. Quietly slipping behind the counter, he waited on the woman himself and then handed the purchase to the salespeople to be wrapped as he went on his way.

Public officials are often criticized for not being accessible to their constituents. They are busy people, and the fault sometimes lies in overprotective assistants who don't want to overburden their bosses with too many visitors. Carl Langford, who had been mayor of Orlando, Florida, the home of Disney World, for many years, frequently admonished his staff to allow people to see him. He claimed he had an "open-door" policy; yet the citizens of his community were blocked by secretaries and administrators when they called.

Finally the mayor found the solution. He removed the door from his office! His aides got the message, and the mayor had a truly open administration from the day his door was symbolically thrown away.

Simply changing one three-letter word can often spell the difference between failure and success in changing people without giving offense or arousing resentment.

Many people begin their criticism with sincere praise followed by the word "but" and ending with a critical statement. For example, in trying to change a child's careless attitude toward studies, we might say, "We're really proud of you, Johnnie, for raising your grades this term. *But* if you had worked harder on your algebra, the results would have been better."

In this case, Johnnie might feel encouraged until he heard the word "but." He might then question the sincerity of the original praise. To him, the praise might seem only to be a contrived lead-in to a critical inference of failure. Credibility would be strained, and we probably would not achieve our objective of changing Johnnie's attitude toward his studies.

This could be easily overcome by changing the word "but" to "and." "We're really proud of you, Johnnie, for raising your grades this term, *and* if you continue the same conscientious efforts next term, your algebra grade can be up with all the others."

Now, Johnnie would accept the praise because there was no follow-up of an inference of failure. We have called his attention to the behavior we wished to change indirectly, and the chances are he will try to live up to our expectations.

Calling attention indirectly to someone's mistakes works wonders with sensitive people who may resent bitterly any direct criticism. Marge Jacob of Woonsocket, Rhode Island, told one of our classes how she convinced some sloppy construction workers to clean up after themselves when they were building additions to her house.

For the first few days of the work, when Mrs. Jacob returned from her job, she noticed that the yard was strewn with the cut ends of lumber. She didn't want to antagonize the builders, because they did excellent work. So after the workers had gone home, she and her children picked up and neatly piled all the lumber debris in a corner. The following morning she called the foreman to one side and said, "I'm really pleased with the way the front lawn was left last night; it is nice and clean and does not offend the neighbors." From that day forward the workers picked up and piled the debris to one side, and the foreman came in each day seeking approval of the condition the lawn was left in after a day's work.

One of the major areas of controversy between members of the army reserves and their regular army trainers is haircuts. The reservists consider themselves civilians (which they are most of the time) and resent having to cut their hair short.

Master Sergeant Harley Kaiser of the 542nd USAR School addressed himself to this problem when he was working with a group of reserve noncommissioned officers. As an old-time regular-army master sergeant, he might have been expected to yell at his troops and threaten them. Instead he chose to make his point indirectly.

"Gentlemen," he started, "you are leaders. You will be most effective when you lead by example. You must be the example for your men to follow. You know what the army regulations say about haircuts. I am going to get my hair cut today, although it is still much shorter than some of yours. You look at yourself in the mirror, and if you feel you need a haircut to be a good example, we'll arrange time for you to visit the post barbershop."

The result was predictable. Several of the candidates did look in the mirror and went to the barbershop that afternoon and received "regulation" haircuts. Sergeant Kaiser commented the next morning that he already could see the development of leadership qualities in some of the members of the squad.

On March 8, 1887, the eloquent Henry Ward Beecher died. The following Sunday, Lyman Abbott was invited to speak in the pulpit left silent by Beecher's passing. Eager to do his best, he wrote, rewrote, and polished his sermon with the meticulous care of a Flaubert. Then he read it to his wife. It was poor—as most written speeches are. She might have said, if she had had less judgment, "Lyman, that is terrible. That'll never do. You'll put people to sleep. It reads like an encyclopedia. You ought to know better than that after all the years you have been preaching. For heaven's sake, why don't you talk like a human being? Why don't you act natural? You'll disgrace yourself if you ever read that stuff."

That's what she *might* have said. And, if she had, you know what would have happened. And she knew too. So, she merely remarked that it would make an excellent article for the *North American Review.* In other words, she praised it and at the same time subtly suggested that it wouldn't do as a speech. Lyman Abbott saw the point, tore up his carefully prepared manuscript, and preached without even using notes.

Don't Call Attention to People's Mistakes Directly

* * *

Most of us have far more courage than we ever dreamed we possessed.

– Dale Carnegie

9

NO ONE LIKES TO TAKE ORDERS

I once had the pleasure of dining with Mrs. Ida Tarbell, the dean of American biographers. When I told her I was writing this book, we began discussing this all-important subject of getting along with people, and she told me that while she was writing her biography of Owen D. Young, she interviewed a man who had sat for three years in the same office with Mr. Young. This man declared that during all that time he had never heard Owen D. Young give a direct order to anyone. He always gave suggestions, not orders. Owen D. Young never said, for example, "Do this or do that," or "Don't do this or don't do that." He would say, "You might consider this," or "Do you think that would work?" Frequently he would say, after he had dictated a letter, "What do you think of this?" In looking over a letter of one of his assistants, he would say, "Maybe if we were to phrase it this way it would be better." He always gave people the opportunity to do things themselves; he never told his assistants to do things; he let them do them, let them learn from their mistakes.

A technique like that makes it easy for a person to correct errors. A technique like that saves a person's pride and gives him or her a feeling of importance. It encourages cooperation instead of rebellion.

Resentment caused by a brash order may last a long time—even if the order was given to correct an obviously bad situation. Dan Santarelli, a teacher at a vocational school in Wyoming, Pennsylvania, told one of our classes how one of his students had blocked the entraceway to one of the school's shops by illegally parking his car in it. One of the other instructors stormed into the classroom and asked in an arrogant tone, "Whose car is blocking the driveway?" When the student who owned the car responded, the instructor screamed: "Move that car and move it right now, or I'll wrap a chain around it and drag it out of there."

Now that student was wrong. The car should not have been parked there. But from that day on, not only did that student resent the instructor's action, but all the students in the class did everything they could to give the instructor a hard time and make his job unpleasant.

How could he have handled it differently? If he had asked in a friendly way, "Whose car is in the driveway?" and then suggested that if it were moved, other cars could get in and out, the student would have gladly moved it and neither he nor his classmates would have been upset and resentful.

Asking questions not only makes an order more palatable; it often stimulates the creativity of the persons whom you ask. People are more likely to accept an order if they have had a part in the decision that caused the order to be issued.

When Ian Macdonald of Johannesburg, South Africa, the general manager of a small manufacturing plant specializing in precision machine parts, had the opportunity to accept a very large order, he was convinced that he would not meet the promised delivery date. The work already scheduled in the shop and the short completion time needed for this order made it seem impossible for him to accept the order.

Instead of pushing his people to accelerate their work and rush the order through, he called everybody together, explained the situation to them, and told them how much it would mean to the company and to them if they could make it possible to produce the order on time. Then he started asking questions:

"Is there anything we can do to handle this order?"

"Can anyone think of different ways to process it through the shop that will make it possible to take the order?"

"Is there any way to adjust our hours or personnel assignments that would help?"

The employees came up with many ideas and insisted that he take the order. They approached it with a "We can do it attitude, and the order was accepted, produced, and delivered on time.

An effective leader will...

Make People Part of the Decision

* * *

An old man was asked what had robbed him of joy in his life. His reply was, "Things that never happened."

– Dale Carnegie

10

LET THE OTHER PERSON SAVE FACE

Years ago the General Electric Company was faced with the delicate task of removing Charles Steinmetz from the head of a department. Steinmetz, a genius of the first magnitude when it came to electricity, was a failure as the head of the calculating department. Yet the company didn't dare offend the man. He was indispensable—and highly sensitive. So they gave him a new title. They made him consulting engineer of the General Electric Company—a new title for work he was already doing—and let someone else head the department.

Steinmetz was happy.

So were the officers of G.E. They had gently maneuvered their most temperamental star, and they had done it without a storm—by letting him save face.

Letting someone save face! How important, how vitally important, that is! And how few of us ever stop to think of it! We ride roughshod over the feelings of others, getting our own way, finding fault, issuing threats, criticizing a child or an employee in front of others, without even considering the hurt to the other person's pride. Whereas a few minutes' thought, a considerate word or two, a genuine understanding of the other person's attitude, would go so far toward alleviating the sting!

Let's remember this the next time we are faced with the distasteful necessity of discharging or reprimanding an employee.

"Firing employees is not much fun. Getting fired is even less fun." (I'm quoting now from a letter written me by Marshall A. Granger, a certified public accountant.) "Our business is mostly seasonal. Therefore we have to let a lot of people go when the income tax rush is over.

"It's a byword in our profession that no one enjoys wielding the ax. Consequently, the custom has developed of getting it over as soon as possible, and usually in the following way: 'Sit down, Mr. Smith. The season's over, and we don't seem to see any more assignments for you. Of course, you understand you were employed only for the busy season anyhow, etc., etc.'

"The effect on these people is one of disappointment and a feeling of being 'let down.' Most of them are in the accounting field for life, and they retain no particular love for the firm that drops them so casually.

"I recently decided to let our seasonal personnel go with a little more tact and consideration. So I call each one in only after carefully thinking over his or her work during the winter. And I've said something like this: 'Mr. Smith, you've done a fine job (if he has). That time we sent you to Newark, you had a tough assignment. You were on the spot, but you came through with flying colors, and we want you to know the firm is proud of you. You've got the stuff—you're going a long way, wherever you're working. This firm believes in you, and is rooting for you, and we don't want you to forget it.'

"Effect? The people go away feeling a lot better about being fired. They don't feel 'let down'. They know that if we had work for them, we'd keep them on. And when we need them again, they come to us with a keen personal affection."

At one session of our course, two class members discussed the negative effects of faultfinding versus the positive effects of letting the other person save face.

Fred Clark of Harrisburg, Pennsylvania, told of an incident that occurred in his company: "At one of our production meetings, a vice-president was asking very pointed questions of one of our production supervisors regarding a production process. His tone of voice was aggressive and aimed at pointing out faulty performance on the part of the supervisor. Not wanting to be embarrassed in front of his peers, the supervisor was evasive in his responses. This caused the vice-president to lose his temper, berate the supervisor, and accuse him of lying.

"Any working relationship that might have existed prior to this encounter was destroyed in a few brief moments. This supervisor, who was basically a good worker, was useless to our company from that time on. A few months later he left our firm and went to work for a competitor, where I understand he is doing a fine job."

Another class member, Anna Mazzone, related how a similar incident had occurred at her job—but what a difference in approach and results! Ms. Mazzone, a marketing specialist for a food packer, was given her first major assignment—the test marketing of a new product. She told the class: "When the results of the test came in, I was devastated. I had made a serious error in my planning, and the entire test had to be done all over again. To make this worse, I had no time to discuss it with my boss before the meeting in which I was to make my report on the project.

"When I was called on to give the report, I was shaking with fright. I had all I could do to keep from breaking down, but I resolved I would not cry and have all those men make remarks about women not being able to handle an assignment because they are too emotional. I made my report briefly and stated that due to an error I would repeat the study before the next meeting. I sat down, expecting my boss to blow up.

"Instead, he thanked me for my work and remarked that it was not unusual for a person to make an error on a new project and that he had confidence that the repeat survey would be accurate and meaningful to the company. He assured me, in front of my colleagues, that he had faith in me and knew I had done my best, and that my lack of experience, not my lack of ability, was the reason for the failure.

"I left that meeting with my head up in the air and with the determination that I would never let that boss of mine down again."

Even if we are right and the other person is definitely wrong, we only destroy ego by causing someone to lose face. Hie legendary French aviation pioneer and author Antoine de Saint-Exupery wrote: "I have no right to say or do anything that diminishes a man in his own eyes. What matters is not what I think of him, but what he thinks of himself. Hurting a man in his dignity is a crime."

Let People Save Face

11

TALK ABOUT YOUR OWN MISTAKES FIRST

My niece, Josephine Carnegie, had come to New York to be my secretary. She was nineteen, had graduated from high school three years previously, and her business experience was a trifle more than zero. She became one of the most proficient secretaries west of Suez, but in the beginning,' she was—well, susceptible to improvement. One day when I started to criticize her, I said to myself: "Just a minute, Dale Carnegie; just a minute. You are twice as old as Josephine. You have ten thousand times as much business experience. How can you possibly expect her to have your viewpoint, your judgment, your initiative—mediocre though they may be? And just a minute, Dale, what were you doing at nineteen? Remember the asinine mistakes and blunders you made? Remember the time you did this ...and that.,.?"

After thinking the matter over, honestly and impartially, I concluded that Josephine's batting average at nineteen was better than mine had been—and that, I'm sorry to confess, isn't paying Josephine much of a compliment.

So after that, when I wanted to call Josephine's attention to a mistake, I used to begin by saying, "You have made a mistake, Josephine, but the Lord knows, it's no worse than many I have made. You were not born with judgment. That comes only with experience, and you are better than I was at your age. I have been guilty of so many stupid, silly things myself, I have very little inclination to criticize you or anyone. But don't you think it would have been wiser if you had done so and so?"

It isn't nearly so difficult to listen to a recital of your faults if the person criticizing begins by humbly admitting that he, too, is far from impeccable.

E. G. Dillistone, an engineer in Brandon, Manitoba, Canada, was having problems with his new secretary. Letters he dictated were coming to his desk for signature with two or three spelling mistakes per page. Mr. Dillistone reported how he handled this:

"Like many engineers, I have not been noted for my excellent English or spelling. For years I have kept a little black thumb-index book for words I had trouble spelling. When it became apparent that merely pointing out the errors was not going to cause my secretary to do more proofreading and dictionary work, I resolved to take another approach. When the next letter came to my attention that had errors in it, I sat down with the typist and said:

"'Somehow this word doesn't look right. It's one of the words I always have had trouble with. That's the reason I started this spelling book of mine. (I opened the book to the appropriate page.) Yes, here it is. I'm very conscious of the spelling now because people do judge us by our letters, and misspellings make us look less professional.

"I don't know whether she copied my system or not, but since that conversation, her frequency of spelling errors has been significantly reduced."

The polished Prince Bernhard von Biilow learned the sharp necessity of doing this back in 1909. Von Biilow was then the imperial chancellor of Germany, and on the throne sat Wilhelm II—Wilhelm, the haughty; Wilhelm, the arrogant; Wilhelm, the last of the German kaisers, building an army and navy that he boasted could whip their weight in wildcats.

Then an astonishing thing happened. The kaiser said things, incredible things, things that rocked the continent and started a series of explosions heard around the world. To make matters worse, the kaiser made silly, egotistical, absurd announcements in public. He made them while he was a guest in England, and he gave his royal permission to have them printed in the *Daily Telegraph*. For example, he declared that he was the only German who felt friendly toward the English; that he was constructing a navy against the menace of Japan; that he, and he alone, had saved England from being humbled in the dust by Russia and France; that it had been *his* campaign plan that enabled England's Lord Roberts to defeat the Boers in South Africa; and so on and on.

No other such amazing words had ever fallen from the lips of a European king in peacetime within a hundred years. The entire continent buzzed with the fury of a hornet's nest. England was incensed. German statesmen were aghast. And in the midst of all this consternation, the kaiser became panicky and suggested to Prince von Biilow, the imperial chancellor, that he take the blame. Yes, he wanted von Biilow to announce that it was all his responsibility, that he had advised his monarch to say these incredible things.

"But Your Majesty," von Biilow protested, "it seems to me utterly impossible that anybody either in Germany or England could suppose me capable of having advised Your Majesty to say any such thing."

The moment those words were out of von Bulow's mouth, he realized he had made a grave mistake. The Kaiser blew up.

"You consider me a donkey," he shouted, "capable of blunders you yourself could never have committed."

Von Bulow knew that he ought to have praised before he condemned; but since it was too late, he did the next best thing. He praised after he had criticized. And it worked a miracle.

"I'm far from suggesting that," he answered respectfully. "Your Majesty surpasses me in many respects; not only, of course, in naval and military knowledge, but above all, in natural science. I have often listened in admiration when Your Majesty explained the barometer, or wireless telegraphy, or the Roentgen rays. I am shamefully ignorant of all branches of natural science, have no notion of chemistry or physics, and am quite incapable of explaining the simplest of natural phenomena. But," von Biilow continued, "in compensation, I possess some historical knowledge and perhaps certain qualities useful in politics, especially in diplomacy."

The kaiser beamed. Von Biilow had praised him. Von Biilow had exalted him and humbled himself. The kaiser could forgive anything after that. "Haven't I always told you," he exclaimed with enthusiasm, "that we complete one another famously? We should stick together, and we will!"

He shook hands with von Biilow, not once, but several times. And later in the day he waxed so enthusiastic that he exclaimed with doubled fists, "If anyone says anything to me against Prince von Biilow, *I shall punch him in the nose*"

Von Biilow saved himself in time—but, canny diplomat that he was, he nevertheless had made one error: he should have *begun* by talking about his own shortcomings and Wilhelm's superiority—not by intimating that the kaiser was a half-wit in need of a guardian.

If a few sentences humbling oneself and praising the other party can turn a haughty, insulted kaiser into a staunch friend, imagine what humility and praise can do for you and me in our daily contacts. Rightly used, they will work veritable miracles in human relations.

Admitting one's own mistakes—even when one hasn't corrected them—can help convince somebody to change his or her behavior. This was illustrated more recently by Clarence Zerhusen of Timonium, Maryland, when he discovered his fifteen-year-old son was experimenting with cigarettes.

"Naturally, I didn't want David to smoke," Mr. Zerhusen told us, "but his mother and I smoked cigarettes; we were giving him a bad example all the time. I explained to Dave how I started smoking at about his age and how the nicotine had gotten the best of me and now it was nearly impossible for me to stop. I reminded him how irritating my cough was and how he had been after me to give up cigarettes not many years before. I didn't exhort him to stop or make threats or warn him about their dangers. All I did was point out how I was hooked on cigarettes and what it had meant to me.

"He thought about it for a while and decided he wouldn't smoke until he had graduated from high school. As the years went by David never did start smoking and has no intention of ever doing so.

"As a result of that conversation I made the decision to stop smoking myself, and with the support of my family, I have succeeded."

Admit to Your Own Faults Before Pointing the Finger at Others

* * *

One of the most tragic things I know about human nature is that all of us tend to put off living. We are all dreaming of some magical rose garden over the horizon instead of enjoying the roses that are blooming outside our windows today.

– Dale Carnegie

PART II
STOP WORRYING

12

FOUR GOOD WORKING HABITS THAT WILL HELP PREVENT FATIGUE AND WORRY

GOOD WORKING HABIT NO. 1

Clear your desk of all papers except those relating to the immediate problem at hand.

Roland L. Williams, President of the Chicago and Northwestern Railway, once said, "A person with his desk piled high with papers on various matters will find his work much easier and more accurate if he clears that desk of all but the immediate problem on hand. I call this good housekeeping, and it is the number-one step toward efficiency."

If you visit the Library of Congress in Washington, D.C., you will find five words painted on the ceiling— five words written by the poet Pope:

"Order is Heaven's first law."

Order ought to be the first law of business, too. But is it? No, the average desk is cluttered up with papers that haven't been looked at for weeks. In fact, the publisher of a New Orleans newspaper once told me that his secretary cleared up one of his desks and found a typewriter that had been missing for two years!

The mere sight of a desk littered with unanswered mail and reports and memos is enough to breed confusion, tension, and worries. It is much worse than that. The constant reminder of "a million things to do and no time to do them" can worry you not only into tension and fatigue, but also into high blood pressure, heart trouble, and stomach ulcers.

Dr. John H. Stokes, professor, Graduate School of Medicine, University of Pennsylvania, read a paper before the National Convention of the American Medical Association—a paper entitled "Functional Neuroses as Complications of Organic Disease." In that paper, Dr. Stokes listed eleven conditions under the title: "What to Look for in the Patient's State of Mind." Here is the first item on that list:

> The sense of must or obligation; the unending stretch of things ahead that simply have to be done.

But how can such an elementary procedure as clearing your desk and making decisions help you avoid this high pressure, this sense of *must*, this sense of an "unending stretch of things ahead" that simply have to be done? Dr. William L. Sadler, the famous psychiatrist, told of a patient who, by using this simple device, avoided a nervous breakdown. The man was an executive in a big Chicago firm. When he came to Dr. Sadler's office, he was tense, nervous, worried. He knew he was heading for a tailspin, but he couldn't quit work. He had to have help.

"While this man was telling me his story," Dr. Sadler says, "my telephone rang. It was the hospital calling; and instead of deferring the matter, I took time right then to come to a decision. I always settle questions, if possible, right on the spot. I had no sooner hung up than the phone rang again. Again an urgent matter, which I took time to discuss. The third interruption came when a colleague of mine came to my office for advice on a patient who was critically ill. When I had finished with him, I turned to my caller and began to apologize for keeping him waiting. But he had brightened up. He had a completely different look on his face."

"Don't apologize, doctor!" this man said to Sadler. "In the last ten minutes, I think I've got a hunch as to what is wrong with me. I'm going back to my office and revise my working habits... But before I go, do you mind if I take a look in your desk?"

Dr. Sadler opened up the drawers of his desk. All empty—except for supplies. "Tell me," said the patient, "where do you keep your unfinished business?"

"Finished!" said Sadler.

"And where do you keep your unanswered mail?"

"Answered!" Sadler told him. "My rule is never to lay down a letter until I have answered it. I dictate the reply to my secretary at once."

Six weeks later, this same executive invited Dr. Sadler to come to his office. He was changed—and so was his desk. He opened the desk drawers to show there was no unfinished business inside of the desk. "Six weeks ago," this executive said, "I had three different desks in two different offices—and was snowed under by my work. I was never finished. After talking to you, I came back here and cleared out a wagonload of reports and old papers. Now I work at one desk, settle things as they come up, and don't have a mountain of unfinished business nagging at me and making me tense and worried. But the most astonishing thing is I've recovered completely. There is nothing wrong anymore with my health!"

Charles Evans Hughes, former Chief Justice of the United States Supreme Court, said: "Men do not die from overwork. They die from dissipation and worry." Yes, from dissipation of their energies—and worry because they never seem to get their work done.

GOOD WORKING HABIT NO. 2

Do things in the order of their importance.

Henry L. Doherty, founder of the nationwide Cities Service Company, said that regardless of how much salary he paid, there were two abilities he found it almost impossible to find.

Those two priceless abilities: first, the ability to think. Second, the ability to do things in the order of their importance.

Charles Luckman, the lad who started from scratch and climbed in twelve years to president of the Pepsodent Company, got a salary of a hundred thousand dollars a year, and made a million dollars besides—that lad declared that he owed much of his success to developing the two abilities that Henry L. Doherty said he found almost impossible to find. Charles Luckman said: "As far back as I can remember, I have gotten up at five o'clock in the morning because I can think better then than any other time—I can think better then and plan my day, plan to do things in the order of their importance."

Frank Bettger, one of America's most successful insurance salesmen, didn't wait until five o'clock in the morning to plan his day. He planned it the night before— set a goal for himself—a goal to sell a certain amount of insurance that day. If he failed, that amount was added to his next day—and so on.

I know from long experience that one is not always able to do things in the order of their importance, but I also know that some kind of plan to do first things first is infinitely better than extemporizing as you go along.

If George Bernard Shaw had not made it a rigid rule to do first things first, he would probably have failed as a writer and might have remained a bank cashier all his life. His plan called for writing five pages each day for nine heartbreaking years, even though he made a total of thirty dollars in those nine years—about a penny a day. Even Robinson Crusoe wrote out a schedule of what he would do each hour of the day.

GOOD WORKING HABIT NO. 3

When you face a problem, solve it then and there if you have the facts necessary to make a decision. Don't keep putting off decisions.

One of my former students, the late H. P. Howell, told me that when he was a member of the board of directors of U.S. Steel, the meetings of the board were often long-drawn-out affairs—many problems were discussed, few decisions were made. The result: each member of the board had to carry home bundles of reports to study.

Finally, Mr. Howell persuaded the board of directors to take up one problem at a time and come to a decision. No procrastination—no putting off. The decision might be to ask for additional facts; it might be to do something or to do nothing. But a decision was reached on each problem before passing on to the next. Mr. Howell told me that the results were striking and salutary: the docket was cleared. The calender was clean. No longer was it necessary for each member to carry home a bundle of reports. No longer was there a worried sense of unresolved problems.

A good rule, not only for the board of directors of U.S. Steel, but for you and me.

GOOD WORKING HABIT NO. 4

Learn to organize, deputize and supervise.

Many business persons are driving themselves to premature graves because they have never learned to delegate responsibility to others, insisting on doing everything themselves. Result: details and confusion overwhelm them. They are driven by a sense of hurry, worry, anxiety and tension. It is hard to learn to delegate responsibilities. I know. It was hard for me, awfully hard. I also know from experience the disasters that can be caused by delegating authority to the wrong people. But difficult as it is to delegate authority, executives must do it if they are to avoid worry, tension and fatigue.

Executives who build up big businesses and don't learn to organize, deputize and supervise usually pop off with heart trouble in their fifties or early sixties—heart trouble caused by tension and worries. Want a specific instance? Look at the death notices in your local paper.

Our fatigue is often caused not by work, but by worry, frustration and resentment.

—Dale Carnegie

* * *

Only the prepared speaker deserves to be confident.

—Dale Carnegie.

13

HOW TO BANISH THE BOREDOM THAT PRODUCES FATIGUE, WORRY AND RESENTMENT

One of the chief causes of fatigue is boredom. To illustrate, let's take the case of Alice, an executive who lives on your street. Alice came home one night utterly exhausted. She *acted* fatigued. She *was* fatigued. She had a headache. She had a backache. She was so exhausted she wanted to go to bed without waiting for dinner. Her mother pleaded... She sat down at the table. The telephone rang. The boy friend! An invitation to a dance! Her eyes sparkled. Her spirits soared. She rushed upstairs, put on her Alice-Blue gown, and danced until three o'clock in the morning; and when she finally did get home, she was not the slightest bit exhausted. She was, in fact, so exhilarated she couldn't fall asleep.

Was Alice really and honestly tired eight hours earlier, when she looked and acted exhausted? Sure she was. She was exhausted because she was bored with her work, perhaps bored with life. There are millions of Alices. You may be one of them.

It is a well-known fact that your emotional attitude usually has far more to do with producing fatigue than has physical exertion. A few years ago, Joseph E. Barmack, Ph.D., published in the *Archives of Psychology* a report of some of his experiments, showing how boredom produces fatigue. Dr. Barmack put a group of students through a series of tests in which, he knew, they could have little interest. The result? The students felt tired and sleepy, complained of headaches and eyestrain, felt irritable. In some cases, even their stomachs were upset. Was it all "imagination"? No. Metabolism tests were taken of these students. These tests showed that the blood pressure of the body and the consumption of oxygen actually decrease when a person is bored, and that the whole metabolism picks up immediately as soon as he begins to feel interest and pleasure in his work!

We rarely get tired when we are doing something interesting and exciting. For example, I recently took a vacation in the Canadian Rockies up around Lake Louise. I spent several days trout fishing along Corral Creek, fighting my way through brush higher than my head, stumbling over logs, struggling through fallen timber—yet after eight hours of this, I was not exhausted. Why? Because I was excited, exhilarated. I had a sense of high achievement: six cut-throat trout. But suppose I had been bored by fishing, then how do you think I would have felt? I would have been worn out by such strenuous work at an altitude of seven thousand feet.

Even in such exhausting activities as mountain climbing, boredom may tire you far more than the strenuous work involved. For example, Mr. S. H. Kingman, president of the Farmers and Mechanics Savings Bank of Minneapolis, told me of an incident that is a perfect illustration of that statement. In July, 1953, the Canadian government asked the Canadian Alpine Club to furnish guides to train the members of the Prince of Wales Rangers in mountain climbing. Mr. Kingman was one of the guides chosen to train these soldiers. He told me how he and the other guides—men ranging from forty-two to fifty-nine years of age—took these young army men on long hikes across glaciers and snow fields and up a sheer cliff of forty feet, where they had to climb with ropes and tiny footholds and precarious handholds. They climbed Michael's Peak, the Vice-President Peak, and other unnamed peaks in the Little Yoho Valley in the Canadian Rockies. After fifteen hours of mountain climbing, these young men, who were in the pink of condition (they had just finished a six-week course in tough Commando training), were utterly exhausted.

Was their fatigue caused by using muscles that had not been hardened by Commando training? Anyone who had ever been through Commando training would hoot at such a ridiculous question! No, they were utterly exhausted because they were bored by mountain climbing. They were so tired that many of them fell asleep without waiting to eat. But the guides—men who were two and three times as old as the soldiers—were they tired? Yes, but not exhausted. The guides ate dinner and stayed up for hours, talking about the day's experiences. They were not exhausted because they were interested.

When Dr. Edward Thorndike of Columbia was conducting experiments in fatigue, he kept young men awake for almost a week by keeping them constantly interested. After much investigation, Dr. Thorndike is reported to have said: "Boredom is the only real cause of diminution of work."

If you are a mental worker, it is seldom the amount of work you do that makes you tired. You may be tired by the amount of work you do *not* do. For example, remember the day last week when you were constantly interrupted. No letters answered. Appointments broken. Trouble here and there. Everything went wrong that day. You accomplished nothing whatever, yet you went home exhausted—and with a splitting head.

The next day everything clicked at the office. You accomplished forty times more than you did the previous day. Yet you went home fresh as a snowy-white gardenia. You have had that experience. So have I.

The lesson to be learned? Just this: our fatigue is often caused not by work, but by worry, frustration, and resentment.

While writing this chapter, I went to see a revival of Jerome Kern's delightful musical comedy *Show Boat.* Captain Andy, captain of the *Cotton Blossom*, says in one of his philosophical interludes: "The lucky folks are the ones that get to do things they enjoy doing." Such folk are lucky because they have more energy, more happiness, less worry and less fatigue. Where your interests are, there is your energy also. Walking ten blocks with a nagging wife or husband can be more fatiguing than walking ten miles with an adoring sweetheart.

And so what? What can you do about it? Well, here is what one stenographer did about it—a stenographer working for an oil company in Tulsa, Oklahoma. For several days each month, she had one of the dullest jobs imaginable: filling out printed forms for oil leases, inserting figures and statistics. This task was so boring that she resolved, in self-defense, to make it interesting. How? She had a daily contest with herself. She counted the number of forms she filled out each morning, and then tried to excel that record in the afternoon. She counted each day's total and tried to better it the next day. Result? She was soon able to fill out more of these dull printed forms than any other stenographer in her division. And what did all this get her? Praise? No... Thanks? No... Promotion? No... Increased pay? No... But it did help to prevent the fatigue that is spawned by boredom. It did give her a mental stimulant. Because she had done her best to make a dull job interesting, she had more energy, more zest, and got far more happiness out of her leisure hours.

I happen to know this story is true, because I married that girl.

Here is the story of another stenographer who found it paid to act *as if* her work were interesting. She used to fight her work. But no more. She is Miss Vallie G. Golden, of Elmhurst, Illinois. Here is her story, as she wrote it to me:

"There are four stenographers in my office and each of us is assigned to take letters from several men. Once in a while we get jammed up in these assignments. One day, when an assistant department head insisted that I do a long letter over, I started to rebel. I tried to point out to him that the letter could be corrected without being retyped—and he retorted that if I didn't do it over, he would find someone else who would! I was absolutely fuming! But as I started to retype this letter, it suddenly occurred to me that there were a lot of other people who would jump at the chance to do the work I was doing. Also, that I was being paid a salary to do just that work. I began to feel better. I suddenly made up my mind to do my work as if I actually enjoyed it—even though I despised it. Then I made this important discovery: if I do my work *as if I* really enjoy it, then I do enjoy it to some extent. I also found I can work faster when I enjoy my work. So there is seldom any need now for me to work overtime. This new attitude of mine gained me the reputation of being a good worker. And when one of the department superintendents needed a private secretary, he asked for me for the job—because, he said, I was willing to do extra work without being sulky! This matter of the power of a changed mental attitude," wrote Miss Golden, "has been a tremendously important discovery to me. It has worked wonders!"

Miss Golden used the wonder-working "as if" philosophy of Professor Hans Vaihinger. He taught us to act "as if" we were happy—and so on.

If you act "as if" you are interested in your job, that bit of acting will tend to make your interest real. It will also tend to decrease your fatigue, your tensions, and your worries.

A few years ago, Harlan A. Howard made a decision that completely altered his life. He resolved to make a dull job interesting—and he certainly had a dull one: washing plates, scrubbing counters, and dishing out ice cream in the high-school lunchroom while the other boys were playing ball or kidding the girls. Harlan Howard despised his job—but since he had to stick to it, he resolved to study ice cream—how it was made, what ingredients were used, why some ice creams were better than others. He studied the chemistry of ice cream, and became a whiz in the high-school chemistry course. He was so interested now in food chemistry that he entered the Massachusetts State College and majored in the field of "food technology." When the New York Cocoa Exchange offered a hundred-dollar prize for the best paper on uses of cocoa and chocolate—a prize open to all college students—who do you suppose won it? ...That's right. Harlan Howard.

When he found it difficult to get a job, he opened a private laboratory in the basement of his home in Amherst, Massachusetts. Shortly after that, a new law was passed. The bacteria in milk had to be counted. Harlan A. Howard was soon counting bacteria for the fourteen milk companies in Amherst—and he had to hire two assistants.

Where will he be twenty-five years from now? Well, the men who are now running the business of food chemistry will be retired then, or dead; and their places will be taken by young lads who are now radiating initiative and enthusiasm. Twenty-five years from now, Harlan A. Howard will probably be one of the leaders in his profession, while some of his classmates to whom he used to sell ice cream over the counter will be sour, unemployed, cussing the government, and complaining that they never had a chance. Harlan A. Howard might never have had a chance, either, if he hadn't resolved to make a dull job interesting.

Years ago, there was another young man who was bored with his dull job of standing at a lathe, turning out bolts in a factory. His first name was Sam. Sam wanted to quit, but he was afraid he couldn't find another job. Since he had to do this dull work, Sam decided he would make it interesting. So he ran a race with the mechanic operating a machine beside him. One of them was to trim off the rough surfaces on his machine, and the other was to trim the bolts down to the proper diameter. They would switch machines occasionally and see who could turn out the most bolts. The foreman, impressed with Sam's speed and accuracy, soon gave him a better job. That was the start of a whole series of promotions. Thirty years later, Sam— Samuel Vauclain— was president of the Baldwin Locomotive Works. But he might have remained a mechanic all his life if he had not resolved to make a dull job interesting.

H. V. Kaltenborn—the famous radio news analyst— once told me how he made a dull job interesting. When he was twenty-two years old, he worked his way across the Atlantic on a cattle boat, feeding and watering the steers. After making a bicycle tour of England, he arrived in Paris, hungry and broke. Pawning his camera for five dollars, he put an ad in the Paris edition of *The New York Herald* and got a job selling stereopticon machines. I can remember those old-fashioned stereoscopes that we used to hold up before our eyes to look at two pictures exactly alike. As we looked, a miracle happened. The two lenses in the stereoscope transformed the two pictures into a single scene with the effect of a third dimension. We saw distance. We got an astounding sense of perspective.

Well, as I was saying, Kaltenborn started out selling these machines from door to door in Paris—and he couldn't speak French. But he earned five thousand dollars in commissions the first year, and made himself one of the highest-paid salesmen in France that year. H. V. Kaltenborn told me that this experience did as much to develop within him the qualities that make for success as did any single year of study at Harvard. Confidence? He told me himself that after that experience, he felt he could have sold *The Congressional Record* to French housewives.

That experience gave him an intimate understanding of French life that later proved invaluable in interpreting, on the radio, European events.

How did he manage to become an expert salesman when he couldn't speak French? Well, he had his employer write out his sales talk in perfect French, and he memorized it. He would ring a doorbell, a housewife would answer, and Kaltenborn would begin repeating his memorized sales talk with an accent so terrible it was funny. He would show the housewife his pictures, and when she asked a question, he would shrug his shoulders and say, "An American ...an American." He would then take off his hat and point to a copy of the sales talk in perfect French that he had pasted in the top of his hat. The housewife would laugh, he would laugh—and show her more pictures. When H. V. Kaltenborn told me about this, he confessed that the job had been far from easy. He told me that there was only one quality that pulled him through: his determination to make the job interesting. Every morning before he started out, he looked into the mirror and gave himself a pep talk: "*Kaltenborn, you have to do this if you want to eat. Since you have to do it—why not have a good time doing it? Why not imagine every time you ring a doorbell that you are an actor before the footlights and that there's an audience out there looking at you? After all, what you are doing is just as funny as something on the stage. So why not put a lot of zest and enthusiasm into it?*"

Mr. Kaltenborn told me that these daily pep talks helped him transform a task that he had once hated and dreaded into an adventure that he liked and made highly profitable.

When I asked Mr. Kaltenborn if he had any advice to give to the young men of America who are eager to succeed, he said: "Yes, go to bat with yourself every morning. We talk a lot about the importance of physical exercise to wake us up out of the half-sleep in which so many of us walk around. But we need, even more, some spiritual and mental exercises every morning to stir us into action. Give yourself a pep talk every day."

Is giving yourself a pep talk every day silly, superficial, childish? No, on the contrary, it is the very essence of sound psychology. "Our life is what our thoughts make it." These words are just as true today as they were eighteen centuries ago when Marcus Aurelius first wrote them in his book on *Meditations:* "Our life is what our thoughts make it."

By talking to yourself every hour of the day, you can direct yourself to think thoughts of courage and happiness, thoughts of power and peace. By talking to yourself about the things you have to be grateful for, you can fill your mind with thoughts that soar and sing.

By thinking the right thoughts, you can make any job less distasteful. Your boss wants you to be interested in your job so that he or she will make more money. But let's forget about what the boss wants. Think only of what getting interested in your job will do for you. Remind yourself that it may double the amount of happiness you get out of life, for you spend about one half of your waking hours at your work, and if you don't find happiness in your work, you may never find it anywhere. Keep reminding yourself that getting interested in your job will take your mind off your worries, and, in the long run, will probably bring promotion and increased pay. Even if it doesn't do that, it will reduce fatigue to a minimum and help you enjoy your hours of leisure.

People rarely succeed unless they have fun in what they are doing.

– Dale Carnegie

Remember happiness doesn't depend upon who you are or what you have; it depends solely on what you think.

– Dale Carnegie

14

FIND YOURSELF AND BE YOURSELF

I have a letter from Mrs. Edith Allred, of Mount Airy, North Carolina: "As a child, I was extremely sensitive and shy," she says in her letter. "I was always overweight and my cheeks made me look even fatter than I was. I had an old-fashioned mother who thought it was foolish to make clothes look pretty. She always said: 'Wide will wear while narrow will tear'; and she dressed me accordingly. I never went parties; never had any fun; and when I went to school, I never joined the other children in outside activities, not even athletics. I was morbidly shy. I felt I was 'different' from everybody else and entirely undesirable.

"When I grew up, I married a man who was several years my senior. But I didn't change. My in-laws were a poised and self-confident family. They were everything I should have been but simply was not. I tried my best to be like them, but I couldn't. Every attempt they made to draw me out of myself only drove me further into my shell. I became nervous and irritable. I avoided all friends. I got so bad I even dreaded the sound of the doorbell ringing! I was a failure. I knew it; and I was afraid my husband would find it out. So, whenever we were in public, I tried to be gay, and overacted my part. I knew I overacted; and I would be miserable for days afterwards. At last I became so unhappy that I could see no point in prolonging my existence. I began to think of suicide."

What happened to change this unhappy woman's life? Just a chance remark!

"A chance remark," Mrs. Allred continued, "transformed my whole life. My mother-in-law was talking one day of how she brought her children up, and she said, 'No matter what happened, I always insisted on their being themselves.' ...'On being themselves.' ...That remark is what did it! In a flash, I realized I had brought all this misery on myself by trying to fit myself into a pattern to which I did not conform.

"I changed overnight! I started being myself. I tried to make a study of my own personality. Tried to find out *what I was.* I studied my strong points. I learned all I could about colors and styles, and dressed in a way that I felt was becoming to me. I reached out to make friends. I joined an organization—a small one at first—and was petrified with fright when they put me on a program. But each time I spoke, I gained a little courage. It took a long while—but today I have more happiness than I ever dreamed possible. In rearing my own children, I have always taught them the lesson I had to learn from such bitter experience: *No matter what happens, always be yourself*"

This problem of being unwilling to be yourself is "as old as history," says Dr. James Gordon Gilkey, "and as universal as human life." This problem of being unwilling to be yourself is the hidden spring behind many neuroses and psychoses and complexes. Angelo Patri has written thirteen books and thousands of syndicated newspaper articles on the subject of child training, and he says: "Nobody is so miserable as he who longs to be somebody and something other than the person he is in body and mind."

This craving to be something you are not is especially rampant in Hollywood. Sam Wood, one of Hollywood's best-known directors, said the greatest headache he has with aspiring young actors is exactly this problem: to make them be themselves. They all want to be second- rate Lana Turners or third-rate Clark Gables. "The public has already had that flavor," Sam Wood keeps telling them; "now it wants something else."

Before he started directing such pictures as *Goodbye, Mr. Chips* and *For Whom the Bell Tolls*, Sam Wood spent years in the real-estate business, developing sales personalities. He declares that the same principles apply in the business world as in the world of moving pictures. You won't get anywhere playing the ape. You can't be a parrot. "Experience has taught me," says Sam Wood, "that it is safest to drop, as quickly as possible, people who pretend to be what they aren't."

I asked Paul Boynton, then employment director for a major oil company, what is the biggest mistake people make in applying for jobs. He ought to know: he has interviewed more than sixty thousand job seekers; and he has written a book entitled *6 Ways to Get a Job.* He replied: "The biggest mistake people make in applying for jobs is in not being themselves. Instead of taking their hair down and being completely frank, they often try to give you the answers they think you want." But it doesn't work, because nobody wants a phony. Nobody ever wants a counterfeit coin.

A certain daughter of a streetcar conductor had to learn that lesson the hard way. She longed to be a singer. But her face was her misfortune. She had a large mouth and protruding buck teeth. When she first sang in public—in a New Jersey night club—she tried to pull down her upper lip to cover her teeth. She tried to act "glamorous." The results? She made herself ridiculous. She was headed for failure.

However, there was a man in this night club who heard the girl sing and thought she had talent. "See here," he said bluntly, "I've been watching your performance and I know what it is you're trying to hide. You're ashamed of your teeth!" The girl was embarrassed, but the man continued, "What of it? Is there any particular crime in having buck teeth? Don't try to hide them! Open your mouth, and the audience will love you when they see you're not ashamed. Besides," he said shrewdly, "those teeth you're trying to hide may make your fortune!"

Cass Daley took his advice and forgot about her teeth. From that time on, she thought only about her audience. She opened her mouth wide and sang with such gusto and enjoyment that she became a top star in movies and radio. Other comedians tried to copy her!

The renowned William James was speaking of people who had never found themselves when he declared that the average person develops only ten percent of his or her latent mental abilities. "Compared to what we ought to be," he wrote, "we are only half awake. We are making use of only a small part of our physical and mental resources. Stating the thing broadly, human individuals thus far live within their limits. They possess powers of various sorts which they habitually fail to use."

You and I have such abilities, so let's not waste a second worrying because we are not like other people. You are something new in this world. Never before, since the beginning of time, has there ever been anybody exactly like you; and never again throughout all the ages to come will there ever be anybody exactly like you again. The science of genetics informs us that you are what you are largely as a result of twenty-four chromosomes contributed by your father and twenty-four chromosomes contributed by your mother. These forty-eight chromosomes comprise everything that determines what you inherit. In each chromosome there may be, says Amram Scheinfeld, "anywhere from scores to hundreds of genes—with a single gene, in some cases, able to change the whole life of an individual." Truly, we are "fearfully and wonderfully" made.

Even after your mother and father met and mated, there was only one chance in 300,000 billion that the person who is specifically you would be born! In other words, if you had 300,000 billion brothers and sisters, they might all have been different from you. Is all this guesswork? No. It is a scientific fact. If you would like to read more about it, consult *You and Heredity*, by Amram Scheinfeld.

I can talk with conviction about this subject of being yourself because I feel deeply about it. I know what I am talking about. I know from bitter and costly experience. To illustrate: when I first came to New York from the cornfields of Missouri, I enrolled in the American Academy of Dramatic Arts. I aspired to be an actor. I had what I thought was a brilliant idea, a shortcut to success, an idea so simple, so foolproof, that I couldn't understand why thousands of ambitious people hadn't already discovered it. It was this: I would study how the famous actors of that day—John Drew, Walter Hampden, and Otis Skinner—got their effects. Then I would imitate the best points of each one of them and make myself into a shining, triumphant combination of all of them. How silly! How absurd! I had to waste years of my life imitating other people before it penetrated through my thick Missouri skull that I had to be myself, and that I couldn't possibly be anyone else.

That distressing experience ought to have taught me a lasting lesson. But it didn't. Not me. I was too dumb. I had to learn it all over again. Several years later, I set out to write what I hoped would be the best book on public speaking for businessmen that had ever been written. I had the same foolish idea about writing this book that I had formerly had about acting: I was going to *borrow* the ideas of a lot of other writers and put them all in one book—a book that would have everything. So I got scores of books on public speaking and spent a year incorporating their ideas into my manuscript. But it finally dawned on me once again that I was playing the fool. This hodgepodge of other men's ideas that I had written was so synthetic, so dull, that no businessman would ever plod through it. So I tossed a year's work into the wastebasket and started all over again. This time I said to myself: "You've got to be Dale Carnegie, with all his faults and limitations. You can't possibly be anybody else." So I quit trying to be a combination of other men, and rolled up my sleeves and did what I should have done in the first place: I wrote a textbook on public speaking out of my own experiences, observations, and convictions as a speaker and a teacher of speaking. I learned—for all time, I hope—the lesson that Sir Walter Raleigh learned. (I am *not* talking about the Sir Walter who threw his coat in the mud for the queen to step on. I am talking about the Sir Walter Raleigh who was professor of English literature at Oxford back in 1904.) "I can't write a book commensurate with Shakespeare," he said, "but I can write a book by me."

Be yourself. Act on the sage advice that Irving Berlin gave the late George Gershwin. When Berlin and Gershwin first met, Berlin was famous but Gershwin was a struggling young composer working for thirty-five dollars a week in Tin Pan Alley. Berlin, impressed by Gershwin's ability, offered Gershwin a job as his musical secretary at almost three times the salary he was then getting. "But don't take the job," Berlin advised. "If you do, you may develop into a second-rate Berlin. But if you insist on being yourself, someday you'll become a first- rate Gershwin."

Gershwin heeded that warning and slowly transformed himself into one of the significant American composers of his generation.

Charlie Chaplin, Will Rogers, Mary Margaret McBride, Gene Autry, and millions of others had to learn the lesson I am trying to hammer home in this chapter. They had to learn the hard way—just as I did.

When Charlie Chaplin first started making films, the director of the picture insisted on Chaplin's imitating a popular German comedian of that day. Charlie Chaplin got nowhere until he acted himself. Bob Hope had a similar experience: spent years in a singing-and-dancing act—and got nowhere until he began to wisecrack and be himself. Will Rogers twirled a rope in vaudeville for years without saying a word. He got nowhere until he discovered his unique gift for humor and began to talk as he twirled his rope.

When Mary Margaret McBride first went on the air, she tried to be an Irish comedian and failed. When she tried to be just what she was—a plain country girl from Missouri—she became one of the most popular radio stars in New York.

When Gene Autry tried to get rid of his Texas accent and dressed like city boys and claimed he was from New York, people merely laughed behind his back. But when he started twanging his banjo and singing cowboy ballads, Gene Autry started out on a career that made him the world's most popular cowboy both in pictures and on the radio.

You are something new in this world. Be glad of it. Make the most of what nature gave you. In the last analysis, all art is autobiographical. You can sing only what you are. You can paint only what you are. You must be what your experiences, your environment, and your heredity have made you. For better or for worse, you must cultivate your own little garden. For better or for worse, you must play your own little instrument in the orchestra of life.

As Emerson said in his essay on "Self-Reliance": "There is a time in every man's education when he arrives at the conviction that envy is ignorance; that imitation is suicide; that he must take himself for better, for worse, as his portion; that though the wide universe is full of good, no kernel of nourishing corn can come to him but through his toil bestowed on that plot of ground which is given to him to till. The power which resides in him is new in nature, and none but he knows what that is which he can do, nor does he know until he has tried."

That is the way Emerson said it. But here is the way a poet—the late Douglas Malloch—said it:

If you can't be a pine on the top of the hill

Be a scrub in the valley—but be
The best little scrub by the side of the rill;

Be a bush, if you can't be a tree.
If you can't be a bush, be a bit of the grass,

And some highway happier make;
If you can't be a muskie, then just be a bass—

But the liveliest bass in the lake!
We can't all be captains, we've got to be crew,

There's something for all of us here.
There's big work to do and there's lesser to do

And the task we must do is the near.
If you can't be a highway, then just be a trail,

If you can't be the sun, be a star;
It isn't by size that you win or you fail—

Be the best of whatever you are!

Speakers who talk about what life has taught them never fail to keep the attention of their listeners.

– Dale Carnegie

* * *

Success is getting what you want. Happiness is wanting what you get.

– Dale Carnegie

15

HOW TO OVERCOME TIREDNESS

Here is an astounding and significant fact: Mental work alone can't make you tired. Sounds absurd. But a few years ago, scientists tried to find out how long the human brain could labor without reaching "a diminished capacity for work," the scientific definition of fatigue. To the amazement of these scientists, they discovered that blood passing through the brain, when it is active, shows no fatigue at all! If you took blood from the veins of a day laborer while he was working, you would find it full of "fatigue toxins" and fatigue products. But if you took a drop of blood from the brain of an Albert Einstein, it would show no fatigue toxins whatever at the end of the day.

So far as the brain is concerned, it can work "as well and as swiftly at the end of eight or even twelve hours of effort as at the beginning." The brain is utterly tireless... So what makes you tired?

Psychiatrists declare that most of our fatigue derives from our mental and emotional attitudes. One of England's most distinguished psychiatrists, J. A. Hadfield, says in his book *The Psychology of Power.* "The greater part of the fatigue from which we suffer is of mental origin; in fact exhaustion of purely physical origin is rare."

One of America's most distinguished psychiatrists, Dr. A. A. Brill, goes even further. He declares, "One hundred percent of the fatigue of the sedentary worker in good health is due to psychological factors, by which we mean emotional factors."

What kinds of emotional factors tire the sedentary (or sitting) worker? Joy? Contentment? No! Never! Boredom, resentment, a feeling of not being appreciated, a feeling of futility, hurry, anxiety, worry—those are the emotional factors that exhaust the sitting worker, make him susceptible to colds, reduce his output, and send him home with a nervous headache. Yes, we get tired because our emotions produce nervous tensions in the body.

The Metropolitan Life Insurance Company pointed that out in a leaflet on fatigue: "Hard work by itself," said this great life insurance company, "seldom causes fatigue which cannot be cured by a good sleep or rest... Worry, tenseness, and emotional upsets are three of the biggest causes of fatigue. Often they are to blame when physical or mental work seems to be the cause... Remember that a tense muscle is a working muscle. Ease up! Save energy for important duties."

Stop now, right where you are, and give yourself a checkup. As you read these lines, are you scowling at the book? Do you feel a strain between the eyes? Are you sitting relaxed in your chair? Or are you hunching up your shoulders? Are the muscles of your face tense? Unless your entire body is as limp and relaxed as an old rag doll, you are at this very moment producing nervous tensions and muscular tensions. *You are producing nervous tensions and nervous fatigue!*

Why do we produce these unnecessary tensions in doing mental work? Daniel W. Josselyn said, "I find that the chief obstacle ...is the almost universal belief that hard work requires a feeling of effort, else it is not well done." So we scowl when we concentrate. We hunch up our shoulders. We call on our muscles to make the motion of *effort*, which in no way assists our brain in its work.

Here is an astonishing and tragic truth: millions of people who wouldn't dream of wasting dollars go right on wasting and squandering their energy with the recklessness of seven drunken sailors in Singapore.

What is the answer to this nervous fatigue? Relax! Relax! Relax! Learn to relax while you are doing your work!

Easy? No. You will probably have to reverse the habits of a lifetime. But it is worth the effort, for it may revolutionize your life! William James said, in his essay "The Gospel of Relaxation": "The American overtension and jerkiness and breathlessness and intensity and agony of expression ...are *bad habits*, nothing more or less." Tension is a habit. Relaxing is a habit. And bad habits can be broken, good habits formed.

How do you relax? Do you start with your mind, or do you start with your nerves? You don't start with either. You always begin to relax with your muscles!

Let's give it a try. To show how it is done, suppose we start with your eyes. Read this paragraph through, and when you've reached the end, lean back, close your eyes, *and say to your eyes* silently, "Let go. Let go. Stop straining, stop frowning. Let go. Let go." Repeat that over and over very slowly for a minute...

Didn't you notice that after a few seconds the muscles of the eyes *began to obey*? Didn't you feel as though some hand had wiped away the tension? Well, incredible as it seems, you have sampled in that one minute the whole key and secret to the art of relaxing. You can do the same thing with the jaw, with the muscles of the face, with the neck, with the shoulders, the whole of the body. But the most important organ of all is the eye. Dr. Edmund Jacobson of the University of Chicago has gone so far as to say that if you can completely relax the muscles of the eyes, you can forget all your troubles! The reason the eyes are so important in relieving nervous tension is that they burn up one fourth of all the nervous energies consumed by the body. That is also why so many people with perfectly sound vision suffer from "eyestrain." They are tensing the eyes.

Vicki Baum, the famous novelist, said that when she was a child, she met an old man who taught her one of the most important lessons she ever learned. She had fallen down and cut her knees and hurt her wrist. The old man picked her up. He had once been a circus clown, and as he brushed her off, he said, "The reason you injured yourself was because you don't know how to relax. You have to pretend you are as limp as a sock, as an old crumpled sock. Come, I'll show you how to do it."

That old man taught Vicki Baum and the other children how to fall, how to do flip-flops, and how to turn somersaults. And always he insisted, "Think of yourself as an old crumpled sock. Then you've *got* to relax!

You can relax in odd moments, almost anywhere you are. Only don't make an effort to relax. *Relaxation is the absence of all tension and effort.* Think ease and relaxation. Begin by thinking relaxation of the muscles of your eyes and your face, saying over and over, "Let go ...let go ... let go and relax." Feel the energy flowing out of your facial muscles to the center of your body. Think of yourself as being as free from tension as a baby.

That is what Galli-Curci, the great soprano, used to do. Helen Jepson told me that she used to see Galli-Curci before a performance, sitting in a chair with all her muscles relaxed and her lower jaw so limp it actually sagged. An excellent practice—it kept her from becoming too nervous before her stage entrance; it prevented fatigue.

Here are four suggestions that will help you learn to relax:

1. Relax in odd moments. Let your body go limp like an old sock. I keep an old, maroon-colored sock on my desk as I work—keep it there as a reminder of how limp I ought to be. If you haven't got a sock, a cat will do. Did you ever pick up a kitten sleeping in the sunshine? If so, both ends sagged like a wet newspaper. Even the yogis in India say that if you want to master the art of relaxation, study the cat. I never saw a tired cat, a cat with a nervous breakdown, or a cat suffering from insomnia, worry, or stomach ulcers. You will probably avoid these disasters if you learn to relax as the cat does.
2. Work, as much as possible, in a comfortable position. Remember that tensions on the body produce aching shoulders and nervous fatigue.

3. Check yourself four or five times a day, and say to yourself, "Am I making my work harder than it actually is? Am I using muscles that have nothing to do with the work I am doing?" This will help you form the *habit* of relaxing, and as Dr. David Harold Fink says, "Among those who know psychology best, it is habits two to one."
4. Test yourself again at the end of the day, by asking yourself, "Just how tired am I? If I am tired, it is not because of the mental work I have done, but the way I have done it." "I measure my accomplishments," said Daniel W. Josselyn, "not by how tired I am at the end of the day, or when irritability proves that my nerves are tired, I know beyond question that it has been an inefficient day both as to quantity and quality." If every businessperson in America would learn that same lesson, our death rate from "hypertension" diseases would drop overnight. And we would stop filling up our sanitariums and asylums with people who have been broken by fatigue and worry.

Take a chance! All life is a chance. The man who goes farthest is generally the one who is willing to do and dare.

– Dale Carnegie

16

DO THIS AND CRITICISM CAN'T HURT YOU

I once interviewed Major General Smedley Butler—old "Gimlet-Eye." Old "Hell-Devil" Butler! Remember him? One of the most colorful, swashbuckling generals who ever commanded the United States Marines.

He told me that when he was young, he was desperately eager to be popular, wanted to make a good impression on everyone. In those days the slightest criticism smarted and stung. But he confessed that thirty years in the Marines had toughened his hide. "I have been berated and insulted," he said, "and denounced as a yellow dog, a snake, and a skunk. I have been cursed by the experts. I have been called every possible combination of unprintable, cuss words in the English language. Bother me? Huh! When I hear somebody cussing me now, I never turn my head to see who is talking."

Maybe old "Gimlet-Eye" Butler was too indifferent to criticism, but one thing is sure: most of us take the little jibes and javelins that are hurled at us far too seriously. I remember the time, years ago, when a reporter from the New York *Sun* attended a demonstration meeting of my adult-education classes and lampooned me and my work. Was I burned up? I took it as a personal insult. I telephoned Gil Hodges, the chairman of the Executive Committee of the *Sun* and practically demanded that he print an article stating the facts—instead of ridicule. I was determined to make the punishment fit the crime.

I am ashamed now of the way I acted. I realize now that half the people who bought the paper never saw that article. Half of those who read it regarded it as a source of innocent merriment. Half of those who gloated over it forgot all about it in a few weeks.

I realize now that people are not thinking about you and me or caring what is said about us. They are thinking about themselves—before breakfast, after breakfast, and right on until ten minutes past midnight. They would be a thousand times more concerned about a slight headache of their own than they would about the news of your death or mine.

Even if you and I are lied about, ridiculed, double- crossed, knifed in the back, and sold down the river by one out of every six of our most intimate friends—let's not indulge in an orgy of self-pity. Instead, let's remind ourselves that that's precisely what happened to Jesus. One of His twelve most intimate friends turned traitor for a bribe that would amount, in our modern money, to about nineteen dollars. Another one of His twelve most intimate friends openly deserted Jesus the moment He got into trouble, and declared three times that he didn't even know Jesus—and swore as he said it. One out of six! That is what happened to Jesus. Why should you and I expect a better score?

I discovered years ago that although I couldn't keep people from criticizing me unjustly, I could do something infinitely more important: I could determine whether I would let the unjust condemnation disturb me.

Let's be clear about this: I am not advocating ignoring all criticism. Far from it. I am talking about *ignoring only unjust criticism.* I once asked Eleanor Roosevelt how she handled unjust criticism—and Allah knows she had a lot of it. She probably had more ardent friends and more violent enemies than any other woman who ever lived in the White House.

She told me that as a young girl she was almost morbidly shy, afraid of what people might say. She was so afraid of criticism that one day she asked her aunt, Theodore Roosevelt's sister, for advice. She said: "Auntie Bye, I want to do so-and-so. But I'm afraid of being criticized."

Teddy Roosevelt's sister looked her in the eye and said: "Never be bothered by what people say, as long as you know in your heart you are right." Eleanor Roosevelt told me that that bit of advice proved to be her Rock of Gibraltar years later, when she was in the White House. She told me that the only way we can avoid all criticism is to be like a Dresden-china figure and stay on a shelf. "Do what you feel in your heart to be right—for you'll be criticized, anyway. You'll be 'damned if you do, and damned if you don't.'" That is her advice.

When the late Matthew C. Brush was president of the American International Corporation, I asked him if he was ever sensitive to criticism, and he replied, "Yes, I was very sensitive to it in my early days. I was eager then to have all the employees in the organization think I was perfect. If they didn't, it worried me. I would try to please first one person who had been sounding off against me; but the very thing I did to patch it up with him would make someone else mad. Then when I tried to fix it up with this person, I would stir up a couple of other bumblebees. I finally discovered that the more I tried to pacify and to smooth over injured feelings in order to escape personal criticism, the more certain I was to increase my enemies. So finally I said to myself, 'If you get your head above the crowd, you're going to be criticized. So get used to the idea.' That helped me tremendously. From that time on I made it a rule to do the very best I could and then put up my old umbrella and let the rain of criticism drain off me instead of run down my neck."

Deems Taylor went a bit further: he let the rain of criticism run down his neck and had a good laugh over it—in public. When he was giving his comments during the intermission of the Sunday-afternoon radio concerts of the New York Philharmonic Symphony Orchestra, one woman wrote him a letter calling him "a liar, a traitor, a snake, and a moron." Mr. Taylor says in his book, *Of Men and Music*. "I have a suspicion that she didn't care for that talk." On the following week's broadcast, Mr. Taylor read this letter over the radio to millions of listeners—and received another letter from the same lady a few days later, "expressing her unaltered opinion," says Mr. Taylor, "that

I was *still* a liar, a traitor, a snake, and a moron." We can't keep from admiring a man who takes criticism like that. We admire his serenity, his unshaken poise, and his sense of humor.

When Charles Schwab was addressing the student body at Princeton, he confessed that one of the most important lessons he had ever learned was taught to him by an old German who worked in Schwab's steel mill. This old German got involved in a hot wartime argument with the other steelworkers, and they tossed him into the river. "When he came into my office," Mr. Schwab said, "covered with mud and water, I asked him what he had said to the men who had thrown him into the river, and he replied, 'I just laughed.'"

Mr. Schwab declared that he had adopted that old German's words as his motto: "Just laugh."

That motto is especially good when you are the victim of unjust criticism. You can answer the man who answers you back, but what can you say to the man who "just laughs"?

Lincoln might have broken under the strain of the Civil War if he hadn't learned the folly of trying to answer all the vitriolic condemnations hurled at him. His description of how he handled his critics has become a literary gem—a classic. General MacArthur had a copy of it hanging above his headquarters desk during the war, and Winston Churchill had a framed copy of it on the wall of his study at Chartwell. It goes like this: "If I were to try to read, much less to answer, all the attacks made on me, this shop might as well be closed for any other business. I do the very best I know how—the very best I can; and I mean to keep on doing so until the end. If the end brings me out all right, then what is said against me won't matter; if the end brings me out wrong, then ten angels swearing I was right would make no difference."

If you want to gather honey, don't kick over the beehive.

– Dale Carnegie

17

WOULD YOU TAKE A MILLION DOLLARS FOR WHAT YOU HAVE?

I have known Harold Abbott for years. He lived in Webb City, Missouri. He used to be my lecture manager. One day he and I met in Kansas City and he drove me down to my farm at Belton, Missouri. During that drive, I asked him how he kept from worrying, and he told me an inspiring story that I shall never forget.

"I used to worry a lot," he said, "but one spring day in 1934, I was walking down West Dougherty Street in Webb City when I saw a sight that banished all my worries. It all happened in ten seconds, but during those ten seconds I learned more about how to live than I had learned in the previous ten years. For two years I had been running a grocery store in Webb City." Harold Abbott said, as he told me the story, "I had not only lost all my savings, but I had incurred debts that took me seven years to pay back. My grocery store had been closed the previous Saturday; and now I was going to the Merchants and Miners Bank to borrow money so I could go to Kansas City to look for a job. I walked like a beaten man. I had lost all my fight and faith. Then suddenly I saw coming down the street a man who had no legs. He was sitting on a little wooden platform equipped with wheels from roller skates. He propelled himself along the street with a block of wood in each hand. I met him just after he had crossed the street and was starting to lift himself up a few inches over the curb to the sidewalk. As he tilted his little wooden platform to an angle, his eyes met mine. He greeted me with a grand smile. 'Good morning, sir. It is a fine morning, isn't it?' he said with spirit. As I stood looking at him, I realized how rich I was. I had two legs. I could walk. I felt ashamed of my self-pity. I said to myself, if he can be happy, cheerful, and confident without legs, I certainly can with legs. I could already feel my chest lifting. I had intended to ask the Merchants and Miners Bank for only one hundred dollars. But now I had courage to ask for *two* hundred. I had intended to say that I wanted to go to Kansas City to *try* to get a job. But now I announced confidently that I wanted to go to Kansas City to *get* a job. I got the loan; and I got the job.

I now have the following words pasted on my bathroom mirror, and I read them every morning as I shave:

I had the blues because I had no shoes,
Until upon the street, I met a man who had no feet.

I once asked Eddie Rickenbacker what was the biggest lesson he had learned from drifting about with his companions in life rafts for twenty-one days, hopelessly lost in the Pacific. "The biggest lesson I learned from that experience," he said, "was that if you have all the fresh water you want to drink and all the food you want to eat, you ought never to complain about anything."

Time ran an article about a sergeant who had been wounded on Guadalcanal. Hit in the throat by a shell fragment, this sergeant had had seven blood transfusions. Writing a note to his doctor, he asked: "Will I live?" The doctor replied: "Yes." He wrote another note, asking, "Will I be able to talk?" Again the answer was yes. He then wrote another note, saying: "Then what in the hell am I worrying about?"

Why don't you stop right now and ask yourself, "What in the hell am I worrying about?" You will probably find that it is comparatively unimportant and insignificant.

About ninety percent of the things in our lives are right and about ten percent are wrong. If we want to be happy, all we have to do is to concentrate on the ninety percent that are right and ignore the ten percent that are wrong. If we want to be worried and bitter and have stomach ulcers, all we have to do is to concentrate on the ten percent that are wrong and ignore the ninety percent that are glorious.

The words "Think and Thank" are inscribed in many of the Cromwellian churches of England. These words ought to be inscribed on our hearts, too: "Think and Thank." Think of all we have to be grateful for, and thank God for all our boons and bounties.

Jonathan Swift, author of *Gulliver's Travels*, was the most devastating pessimist in English literature. He was so sorry that he had been born that he wore black and fasted on his birthdays; yet, in his despair, this supreme pessimist of English literature praised the great health- giving powers of cheerfulness and happiness. "The best doctors in the world," he declared, "are Doctor Diet, Doctor Quiet, and Doctor Merryman."

You and I may have the services of "Doctor Merryman" free every day by keeping our attention fixed on all the incredible riches we possess—riches exceeding by far the fabled treasures of Ali Baba. Would you sell both your eyes for a billion dollars? What would you take for your two legs? Your hands? Your hearing? Your children? Your family? Add up your assets, and you will find that you won't sell what you have for all the gold ever amassed by the Rockefellers, the Fords, and the Morgans combined.

But do we appreciate all this? Ah, no. As Schopenhauer said: "We seldom think of what we have but always of what we lack." Yes, the tendency to "seldom think of what we have but always of what we lack" is the greatest tragedy on earth. It has probably caused more misery than all the wars and diseases in history.

It caused John Palmer to turn "from a regular guy into an old grouch," and almost wrecked his home. I know because he told me so.

Mr. Palmer lived in Paterson, New Jersey. "Shortly after I returned from the Army," he said, "I started in business for myself. I worked hard day and night. Things were going nicely. Then trouble started. I couldn't get parts and materials. I was afraid I would have to give up my business. I worried so much that I changed from a regular guy into an old grouch. I became so sour and cross that—well, I didn't know it then but I now realize that I came very near to losing my happy home. Then one day a young, disabled veteran who works for me said, 'Johnny, you ought to be ashamed of yourself. You take on as if you were the only person in the world with troubles. Suppose you do have to shut up shop for a while—so what? You can start up again when things get normal. You've got a lot to be thankful for. Yet you are always growling. Boy, how I wish I were in your shoes! Look at me. I've got only one arm, and half of my face is shot away, and yet I am not complaining. If you don't stop your growling and grumbling, you will lose not only your business, but also your health, your home, and your friends!'

"Those remarks stopped me dead in my tracks. They made me realize how well off I was. I resolved then and there that I would change and be my old self again—and I did."

A friend of mine, Lucile Blake, had to tremble on the edge of tragedy before she learned to be happy about what she had instead of worrying over what she lacked.

I met Lucile years ago, when we were both studying short-story writing in the Columbia University School of Journalism. Some years ago, she got the shock of her life. She was living then in Tucson, Arizona. She had—well, here is the story as she told it to me:

"I had been living in a whirl: studying the organ at the University of Arizona, conducting a speech clinic in town, and teaching a class in musical appreciation at the Desert Willow Ranch, where I was staying. I was going in for parties, dances, horseback rides under the stars. One morning I collapsed. My heart! 'You will have to lie in bed for a year of complete rest,' the doctor said. He didn't encourage me to believe I would ever be strong again.

"In bed for a year! To be an invalid—perhaps to die! I was terror-stricken! Why did all this have to happen to me? What had I done to deserve it? I wept and wailed. I was bitter and rebellious. But I did go to bed as the doctor advised. A neighbor of mine, Mr.

Rudolf, an artist, said to me, 'You think now that spending a year in bed will be a tragedy. But it won't be. You will have time to think and get acquainted with yourself. You will make more spiritual growth in these next few months than you have made during all your previous life.' I became calmer, and tried to develop a new sense of values. I read books of inspiration. One day I heard a radio commentator say: 'You can express only what is in your own consciousness.' I had heard words like these many times before, but now they reached down inside me and took root. I resolved to think only the thoughts I wanted to live by: thoughts of joy, happiness, health. I forced myself each morning, as soon as I awoke, to go over all the things I had to be grateful for. No pain. A lovely young daughter. My eyesight. My hearing. Lovely music on the radio. Time to read. Good food. Good friends. I was so cheerful and had so many visitors that the doctor put up a sign saying that only one visitor at a time would be allowed in my cabin—and only at certain hours.

"Many years have passed since then, and I now lead a full, active life. I am deeply grateful now for that year I spent in bed. It was the most valuable and the happiest year I spent in Arizona. The habit I formed then of counting my blessings each morning still remains with me. It is one of my most precious possessions. I am ashamed to realize that I never really learned to live until I feared I was going to die."

My dear Lucile Blake, you may not realize it, but you learned the same lesson that Dr. Samuel Johnson learned two hundred years ago. "The habit of looking on the best side of every event," said Dr. Johnson, "is worth more than a thousand pounds a year."

Those words were uttered, mind you, not by a professional optimist, but by a man who had known anxiety, rags, and hunger for twenty years—and finally became one of the most eminent writers of his generation and the most celebrated conversationalist of all time.

Logan Pearsall Smith packed a lot of wisdom into a few words when he said: "There are two things to aim at in life: first, to get what you want; and, after that, to enjoy it. Only the wisest of mankind achieve the second."

Would you like to know how to make even dishwashing at the kitchen sink a thrilling experience? If so, read an inspiring book of incredible courage by Borghild Dahl. It is called *I Wanted to See.*

This book was written by a woman who was practically blind for half a century. "I had only one eye," she writes, "and it was so covered with dense scars that I had to do all my seeing through one small opening in the left of the eye. I could see a book only by holding it up close to my face and by straining my one eye as hard as I could to the left."

But she refused to be pitied, refused to be considered "different." As a child, she wanted to play hopscotch with other children, but she couldn't see the markings. So after the other children had gone home, she got down on the ground and crawled along with her eyes near the marks. She memorized every bit of the ground where she and her friends played and soon became an expert at running games. She did her reading at home, holding a book of large print so close to her eyes that her eyelashes brushed the pages. She earned two college degrees: a B.A. from the University of Minnesota and a Master of Arts from Columbia University.

She started teaching in the tiny village of Twin Valley, Minnesota, and rose until she became professor of journalism and literature at Augustana College in Sioux Falls, South Dakota. She taught there for thirteen years, lecturing before women's clubs and giving radio talks about books and authors. "In the back of my mind," she writes, "there had always lurked a fear of total blindness. In order to overcome this, I had adopted a cheerful, almost hilarious, attitude toward life."

Then in 1943, when she was fifty-two years old, a miracle happened: an operation at the famous Mayo Clinic. She could now see forty times as well as she had ever been able to see before.

A new and exciting world of loveliness opened before her. She now found it thrilling even to wash dishes in the kitchen sink. "I begin to play with the white fluffy suds in the dishpan," she writes. "I dip my hands into them and I pick up a ball of tiny soap bubbles. I hold them up against the light, and in each of them I can see the brilliant colors of a miniature rainbow."

As she looked through the window above the kitchen sink, she saw "the flapping gray-black wings of the sparrows flying through the thick, falling snow."

She found such ecstasy looking at the soap bubbles and sparrows that she closed her book with these words: "'Dear Lord,' I whisper. Our Father in Heaven, I thank Thee. I thank Thee.'"

Imagine thanking God because you can wash dishes and see rainbows in bubbles and sparrows flying through the snow!

You and I ought to be ashamed of ourselves. All the days of our years we have been living in a fairyland of beauty, but we have been too blind to see, too satiated to enjoy.

Tell the audience what you're going to say, say it; then tell them what you've said.

– Dale Carnegie

* * *

The essence of all art is to have pleasure in giving pleasure.

– Dale Carnegie

www.ingramcontent.com/pod-product-compliance
Lightning Source LLC
LaVergne TN
LVHW101923220826
846093LV00009B/344

* 9 7 8 9 3 5 8 0 4 9 8 1 7 *